The Illustrated Book of SOUNDS & THEIR SPELLING PATTERNS

The right-brained approach to teaching word structure in 20 minutes a day

For kindergarten through adult

Sarah K Major, M.Ed.

CHILD1ST
PUBLICATIONS LLC

For teaching resources for visual & other right-brained learners, visit

www.child1st.com

The Illustrated Book of Sounds & Their Spelling Patterns, 3rd Edition

Grades: Kindergarten through adult

© 2018 Sarah K Major

ISBN: 978-1-947484-08-5

Printed in the United States of America

All rights reserved. The reproduction of any part of this book for an entire school or school system or for commercial use is strictly prohibited. No form of this work may be reproduced, transmitted, or recorded without written permission from the publisher. The pages in this book bearing a copyright line may be reproduced for instructional or administrative use (not for resale).

To request more information regarding the copyright policy, contact:

Child1st Publications

800-881-0912 (phone)

888-886-1636 (fax)

info@child1st.com

www.child1st.com

THE ILLUSTRATED BOOK OF SOUNDS & THEIR SPELLING PATTERNS

There are a finite number of sounds that make up all the words in our language. With *The Illustrated Book of Sounds & Their Spelling Patterns*, students will learn to read and spell those sounds that are the building blocks of all words. *The Illustrated Book of Sounds & Their Spelling Patterns* replaces ineffective memorization of words, phonics rules, or decoding with kid-friendly, brain-friendly patterns and visuals. Students are engaged in listening to sounds, finding patterns, and learning through cartoons and story bytes. *The Illustrated Book of Sounds & Their Spelling Patterns* demystifies reading and spelling by giving students the tools they need to identify unknown, difficult words with ease.

The Illustrated Book of Sounds & Their Spelling Patterns has been tested in classrooms from regular classes to resource and special education settings, from whole group to small group, and with children in grades one through middle school. *The Illustrated Book of Sounds & Their Spelling Patterns* empowers teachers and parents to provide differentiated instruction to every student regardless of their ability level.

The best news about *The Illustrated Book of Sounds & Their Spelling Patterns* is that it can be incorporated into any existing curriculum in 15-20 minutes a day in place of the spelling lesson. Learning becomes fun and lasting, producing fluent readers. *The Illustrated Book of Sounds & Their Spelling Patterns* is also teacher-friendly. Once you are familiar with the approach, your work is done! Simply present each lesson, review 10-15 minutes for the next three days, then assess on the 5th day. This cycle is repeated as you progress through the book.

This book is a perfect companion to SnapWords® and to the Easy-for-Me™ Reading Program.

TABLE OF CONTENTS

Table of Contents iv
Fundamentals vii
Finger mapping ix
Daily Routine xiii
Sound Spellings and Their Keywords Chart xiv
Using Keywords Effectively xv
Tracking Sheet xvi
Teaching Notes xviii

SOUNDS BY TEACHING SEQUENCE

Before beginning to teach this sequence of lessons, please take time to study the section called "Fundamentals" on page vii. This section will be your map to success. Also, be sure to follow the Daily Routine from page xiii. It will be so tempting to teach these lessons from a traditional perspective in which we have children spell the words repeatedly in an attempt to have them memorize how to spell each word. It is far more effective to let the child's visual brain "do its thing" because visual learning is easier, quicker, and more memorable. If you rely on the principles in Fundamentals and in the Daily Routine, you will not fail!

Lesson	Page
Short A, Level 1	1
Short E, Level 1	2
Short I, Level 1	3
Short O, Level 1	4
Short U, Level 1	5
Short A, Level 2	6
Digraph SH, Level 1	7
Digraph TH, Level 1	8
Digraph CH, Level 1	9
Short E, Level 2	10
Short I, Level 2	11
NG & NK, Level 1	12
Short O, Level 2	13
Long A, Level 1	14
Long A, Level 2	15
Long E, Level 1	16
Final Y, /Long I/ & /Long E/, Level 1	17
Long I, Level 1	18
Long I, Level 2	19
Long I, Level 3	20
Long I, Level 4	21
/L/, Level 1	22
Long O, Level 1	23
Long O, Level 2	24
Long O, Level 3	25
Long U	26
ŌŌ, Level 1	27
ŌŌ, Level 2	28
ŎŎ, Level 1	29
/OI/, Level 1	30
/OW/, Level 1	31
/ER/, Level 1	32
/ER/, Level 2	33
/AR/, Level 1	34
/AR/, Level 2	35
/K/, Level 1	36
/K/ & /KW/, Level 2	37
Short E, Level 3	38
Short O, Level 3	39
Short U, Level 2	40
/AIR/, Level 1	41
/EAR/, Level 1	42
/EAR/, Level 2	43
/OR/, Level 1	44
/OR/, Level 2	45
Soft C & G, Level 1	46
Soft C & G, Level 2	47
Double Consonants, Level 1	48
Double Consonants, Level 2	49
Long E, Level 2	50
Long E, Level 3	51
Long O, Level 4	52
Digraph TH, Level 2	53
Digraph CH, Level 2	54
Digraph WH, Level 1	55
ŌŌ, Level 3	56
ŎŎ, Level 2	57
/OI/, Level 2	58
/OW/, Level 2	59
Schwa /UH/	60
NG & NK, Level 2	61
Final Y /Long E/, Level 2	62
/ER/, Level 3	63
/OR/, Level 3	64
/F/, Level 1	65
/L/, Level 2	66
/R/, Level 1	67
Past Tense, /T/, /D/, /ED/, Level 1	68
Past Tense, /T/, /D/, /ED/, Level 2	69
Plurals, +S, +ES, Level 1	70
Short O, Level 4	71
Short U, Level 3	72
Long A, Level 3	73
Long A, Level 4	74
Homophones, Level 1	75
Homophones, Level 2	76
Long E, Level 4	77
Long E, Level 5	78
Digraph WH, Level 2	79
/OW/, Level 3	80
/OW/, Level 4	81
/ER/, Level 4	82
/ER/, Level 5	83
/AR/, Level 3	84
/AIR/, Level 2	85
/AIR/, Level 3	86
/OR/, Level 4	87
Soft C & G, Level 3	88
Soft C & G, Level 4	89
/F/, Level 2	90
/G/	91
/L/, Level 3	92
/L/, Level 4	93
/M/	94
/N/	95
/T/, Level 1	96
/Z/	97
OUGH, Level 1	98
OUGH, Level 2	99
Past Tense, /T/, /D/, /ED/, Level 3	100
Plurals, +IES, +S, +ES, Level 2	101

Special Endings:

+N, +EN	102
+ISH, +IST, +IZE	103
+SURE, +TURE	104
+CIA, +TIA, +SIA	105
Homophones, Level 3	106
Short I, Level 3	107
Digraph SH, Level 2	108
Digraph SH, Level 3	109
ŌŌ, Level 4	110
ŌŌ, Level 5	111
/OI/, Level 3	112
/OI/, Level 4	113

Double Consonants, Level 3	114
Double Consonants, Level 4	115
/F/, Level 3	116
/F/, Level 4	117
/R/, Level 2	118
/R/, Level 3	119
/S/, Level 1	120
/S/, Level 2	121
/T/, Level 2	122
Plurals, Level 3	123
Plurals, Level 4	124

Special Endings:

+ER	125
+OR	126
+ION, +IAN	127
+SION, +TION, +CIAN	128
+MENT, +ATE, +NESS	129
+ANT	130
+ENT, +EER	131
+ITY, +TY	132
+ARY	133
+ALLY, +LY, +WARD	134
+OUS	135
+CIOUS, +SCIOUS, +TIOUS, +XIOUS	136
+IOUS	137
+EOUS, +UOUS	138

Y, W, V, P, B, D not included because the sounds of these consonants are not made with other letters.
Ex: /B/ is always spelled either B or BB.

The only exception to this is the sound for /H/, which is spelled H and WH as in "who."

SOUNDS BY CATEGORY

In this Table of Contents, you will see the lessons laid out by sound rather than by teaching sequence. This format will allow you to quickly locate all the lessons that relate to an individual sound. Because some sounds have multiple levels of difficulty, it might be helpful to see all the levels before beginning to teach. The sounds taught in this book correlate with our Sound Spelling Display Cards and our Sound Spelling Teaching Cards. While *Sounds & Their Spelling Patterns* is a stand-alone resource, you may choose to use the Display and Teaching Cards to teach each sound spelling, and then use this book for student practice.

Short Vowel Spellings:

a
   level 1 1
   level 2 6
e
   level 1 2
   level 2 10
   level 3 38
i
   level 1 3
   level 2 11
   level 3 107
o
   level 1 4
   level 2 13
   level 3 39
   level 4 71
u
   level 1 5
   level 2 40
   level 3 72

Long Vowel Spellings:

a
   level 1 14
   level 2 15
   level 3 73
   level 4 74
e
   level 1 16
   level 2 50
   level 3 51
   level 4 77
   level 5 78
i
   level 1 18
   level 2 19
   level 3 20
   level 4 21
o
   level 1 23
   level 2 24
   level 3 25
   level 4 52
u 26

Digraphs:

sh
   level 1 7
   level 2 108
   level 3 109
th
   level 1 8
   level 2 53
ch
   level 1 9
   level 2 54
wh
   level 1 55
   level 2 79

Long ŌŌ & Short ŎŎ:

Long ŌŌ
   level 1 27
   level 2 28
   level 3 56
   level 4 110
   level 5 111
Short ŎŎ
   level 1 29
   level 2 57

v

Diphthongs & NG, NK:
oi
   level 1 30
   level 2 58
   level 3 112
   level 4 113
ow
   level 1 31
   level 2 59
   level 3 80
   level 4 81
ng, nk
   level 1 12
   level 2 61

Final Y:
/Long I/ & /Long E/
   level 1 17
/Long E/
   level 2 62

Bossy R:
/er/
   level 1 32
   level 2 33
   level 3 63
   level 4 82
   level 5 83
/ar/
   level 1 34
   level 2 35
   level 3 84
/or/
   level 1 44
   level 2 45
   level 3 64
   level 4 87
/air/
   level 1 41
   level 2 85
   level 3 86
/ear/
   level 1 42
   level 2 43

Soft C & G:
   level 1 46
   level 2 47
   level 3 88
   level 4 89

Double Consonants:
   level 1 48
   level 2 49
   level 3 114
   level 4 115

Schwa
/UH/ 60

Consonant Spellings:
/F/
   level 1 65
   level 2 90
   level 3 116
   level 4 117
/G/ 91
/K/ & /KW/
   level 1 36
   level 2 37
/L/
   level 1 22
   level 2 66
   level 3 92
   level 4 93
/M/ 94
/N/ 95
/R/
   level 1 67
   level 2 118
   level 3 119
/S/
   level 1 120
   level 2 121
/T/
   level 1 96
   level 2 122
/Z/ 97

OUGH:
   level 1 98
   level 2 99

Past Tense, /T/, /D/, /ED/ :
   level 1 68
   level 2 69
   level 3 100

Plurals:
+S and +ES
   level 1 70
+IES, +S, and +ES
   level 2 101
   level 3 123
   level 4 124

Special Endings:
+N, +EN 102
+ISH, +IST, +IZE 103
+SURE, +TURE 104
+CIA, +TIA, +SIA 105
+ER 125
+OR 126
+ION, +IAN 127
+SION, +TION, +CIAN 128
+MENT, +ATE, +NESS 129
+ANT 130
+ENT, +EER 131
+ITY, +TY 132
+ARY 133
+ALLY, +LY, +WARD 134
+OUS 135
+CIOUS, +SCIOUS, +TIOUS, +XIOUS 136
+IOUS 137
+EOUS, +UOUS 138

Homophones:
   level 1 75
   level 2 76
   level 3 106

Find companion products at child1st.com!

Sound Spelling Teaching Cards   Sound Spelling Display Cards

FUNDAMENTALS

As you progress through the units, there are some fundamental practices that will help as you guide your students toward a better understanding of how words are constructed. The bulk of your preparation for teaching will happen in this preliminary stage of incorporating these elements into your practice.

Teach words as sounds, not a series of letters. For many learners, it is essential that we focus on the sounds that make words rather than spelling words by calling out the letter names. For example, when discussing the word "father," you will not spell the word ("eff, aye, tee, aich, ee, are") but you will speak the four sounds in the word: "ff, ahh, th, er." There are six letters but only four sounds. Visual learners need to learn to focus on the sequence of <u>sounds</u> they hear in words.

Teach one sound at a time. There are a finite number of sounds in our language. These can be mastered and then used to create an infinite number of words.

Teach all the ways to spell a sound at one time. These various sound spellings are presented together so students will see how many ways there are to spell each sound. This practice eliminates a lot of confusion for the students when presented with unknown words.

For example, "short o" as in "pot" or "octopus" actually can be spelled six ways:
- o as in pot
- au as in author, august, because
- aw as in saw, awesome, lawn
- augh as in daughter, caught, naughty
- ough as in ought, brought, bought, fought, thought
- a as in father, want, water

Conversely, a cluster of letters may represent several sounds:
- ough says o as in fought
- ough says oh as in though
- ough says ow as in bough, drought, slough
- ough says uf as in rough, tough, enough
- ough say ooo as in through
- ough says off as in cough

Color-code the target sound in each lesson. Color-coding is a powerful visual tool that helps many struggling students recognize the sound pattern in all the related words. For instance, in the "aw" lesson, the students will highlight, in yellow, that spelling in all the words: "fawn, lawn, dawn, yawn, law, draw, straw, crawl." All that is needed is a highlighter or yellow crayon and thirty seconds the first time the lesson is introduced. Explain that when they read the AW words, everything that is yellow says, "AW."

Practice daily with whiteboard and marker. Teachers gain instant feedback on each student's understanding of the lesson, while children become active participants and are compelled to learn "from the brain out" rather than being passive listeners with marginal learning benefits. Children are given the opportunity to learn the structure of words using all their modalities. They hear the word, orally break it into sounds, and then they repeat the sounds as they represent those sounds with letters on their whiteboards. They are hearing, speaking, moving, and seeing the lesson. About fifteen minutes each day of whiteboard practice is essential for mastery of these lessons. *See "Helpful hints" at the end of this section.

Group words with same sound spelling in sentences. This practice provides a framework that helps a child easily remember which words contain a particular sound spelling. Because sentences are illustrated with cartoons, the child's learning is nearly instant. The brain can record and recall a picture far more easily than a memorized sequence of letters. The sentences also enhance the students' understanding of the meaning of each word. The story bytes and cartoons engage students in their learning.

Use fingermapping as a framework for sound sequence. Fingermapping is an exciting and very effective practice that helps beginners or visual learners see a map of the the sequence of the sounds they are hearing. Many new and struggling readers reverse, insert, or omit sounds. Fingermapping prevents all this by providing students with a visual map, or structure, for each word. There are many students who simply cannot correctly write new words until they see the fingermap. One look at the map, and they can correctly sound and write the word. Over time, the reliance on a visual fingermap diminishes totally, but in the beginning, for some children, the visual structure is the only means by which they correctly sequence sounds and letters.

A recurring comment made by teachers first introduced to fingermapping is, "Oh, I could never learn how to do that!" But like any new skill we learn, the practice of fingermapping, while it is strange in the beginning, will become automatic and easy to use. The value to students who need it far outweighs the difficulties. A detailed explanation of fingermapping follows.

*Helpful hints:

You do not have to purchase costly white boards from a teaching supply store. If you buy one 4'x8' shower board from a building supply store, you can have them cut the board into pieces that are 12" tall and 16" wide. One shower board will make 24 student boards. You will have to purchase markers, but you can buy bundles of cheap, white tube socks to use for erasers. The children keep their markers inside the tube socks for storing in their desks, and during the lesson, the tube socks are wonderful erasers. Take them home periodically and wash in a bleach solution.

Guidelines to set in place from the beginning include no doodling with markers during whiteboard time. Every child I have met loves markers on whiteboards and often become distracted by drawing lines and grids, or decorating their words with flowery sorts of lines. While I am all for illustration for deepening learning, I don't encourage this practice during our whiteboard lesson because the children are better able to stay focused on the lesson.

FINGERMAPPING

Fingermapping is a practice I developed as I worked with Title 1 students in grades K - 7 in reading. It emerged out of repeated attempts to find something visual and concrete that would help my students grasp the structure and order of sound spellings. Fingermapping provides a visual map of words just like a map provides a visual for oral directions.

The teacher does the fingermapping as they introduce each word to the students, then teacher and students all sound out the word together. My suggestion is that at least in the beginning, a teacher practice finger mapping each list of words before presenting the lesson. Over time, the action of fingermapping will become automatic.

1. Basics of Fingermapping

For words containing up to five letters, the teacher will use the left hand, held up with palm facing the students (*figure 1*):

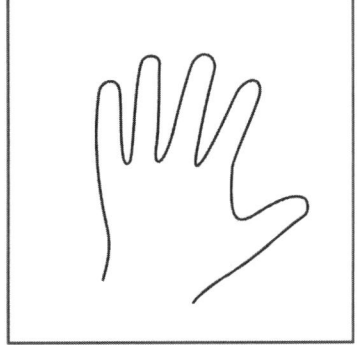

Figure 1

From this point on, thumb is finger #1, pointer is finger #2, "tall man" is finger #3, ring is finger #4, and pinkie is finger #5. Each finger represents one letter. The illustrations in this section will show what you see as you are fingermapping. Note that the words will appear backwards to you.

In a word such as "cat," there are three letters and three distinct sounds: "c – a – t" so the map would look like this (see *figure 2*). The only time fingers are displayed touching each other is when two or more letters represent one sound ("igh" in night or "ai" in rain).

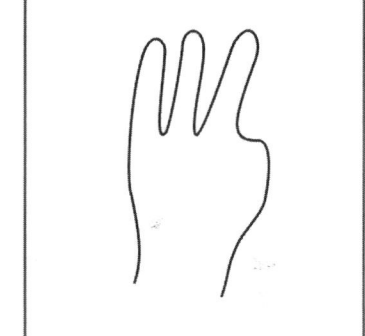

Figure 2

When you present the lesson for the first time, follow this sequence:

1. Say, "When I say, 'Ready,' that is your signal that we are going to start a new word. You will look at me, listen as I say the word, then listen as I sound it. Let me model for you."

2. Say, "Cat. Cat has three letters (hold up your three fingers as in figure 2) and three sounds." Point to the tip of your tall man finger as you sound C (not letter name). Point to the tip of your ring finger as you sound A, and to the tip of your pinkie finger as you sound T.

3. "Now you sound out 'cat' with me." Repeat sounding as you point to each finger tip with students joining you. Remember, you are mapping backwards to YOU so that the word map will appear correct to the students (*figure 3*).

4. Say, "Now sound out 'cat' again, but this time, write the sounds as you say them on your whiteboard. When you say 'c,' write it, when you say 'a,' write it, and when you say 't,' write it." Be sure you do not say letter names, but rather sounds: 'c' as in cave, 'a' as in ant, and 't' as in top. Some students will readily sound and write, while others will appear determined to NOT sound. It is critical for all students to sound as they write, so they will all place the correct sounds in the right sequence.

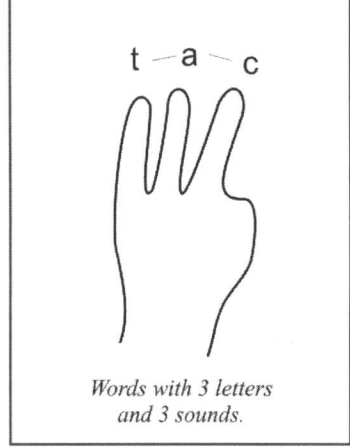

Words with 3 letters and 3 sounds.

Figure 3

5. Do a quick visual check of whiteboards and then say, "Ready," and repeat the steps with the next word.

In time, this process should evolve into crisp, one-word directions:
- Say, "Ready?"
- Say, "The word is, 'sand.'"
- Say, "/s/ /a/ /n/ /d/."
- Say, "Sound it with me."
- All together say, "/s/ /a/ /n/ /d/."
- Say, "Sound and write." (Students will sound and write on whiteboards.)
- Do a rapid visual check.
- Correct if needed by fingermapping and identifying the sound for each finger or finger cluster.
- Repeat process for next word.

Do all within your power to break students of the habit of looking at the printed word and then copying it to their whiteboards. If children rely on copying words they see, they will miss the power of hearing and representing sounds. Insist that all of them can hear the sounds and write what they hear. If you notice that there are problems with representing the words with letters (whether omissions, reversals, or additions), show them the fingermap again.

2. Fingermapping Blends

Remember that each finger represents a letter. When fingermapping "flag" or "stop" you will use four fingers, # 2-5, each separate from the other (*figure 4*). Blends such as "fl" or "st" are two distinct sounds, not one. Blends do not need to be taught separately because children can distinctly hear the sounds of each letter in the blend. Not so with digraphs (sh) or diphthongs (oi) which are combinations of letters that form a new sound together.

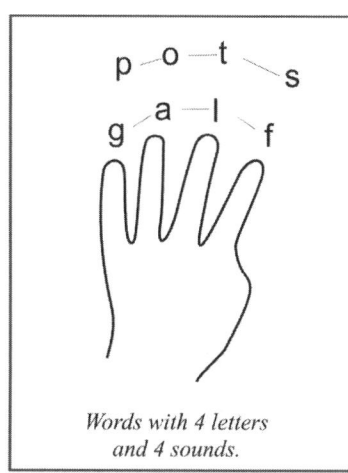

Words with 4 letters and 4 sounds.

Figure 4

When finger mapping and sounding "flag," hold up four fingers, and while pointing to each fingertip, say four separate sounds: /f/, /l/, /a/, /g/. The map will be the same for any other four letter word with four distinct, separate sounds: stop, sand, stem, pant, bent, tent, etc.

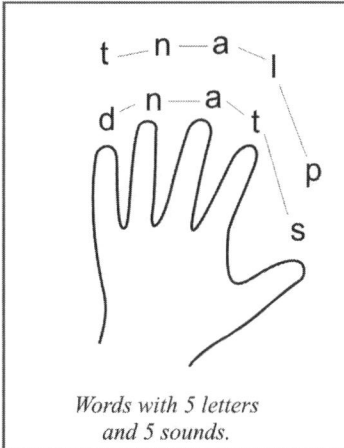

Words with 5 letters and 5 sounds.

Figure 5

Words such as "stand," "plant," and "frank" require five fingers, each separate from the other (*figure 5*). Again, in those words, despite initial and final consonant blends, each sound may be heard distinctly, so each sound requires one finger in mapping.

3. Fingermapping Sounds With Multiple Letters

Vowel teams require more than one letter to produce. For example, in "play" it takes both a and y to make the long a sound. In "rain" the combination of a and i produces the sound of long a. In "road" and "read," the vowel teams of oa and ea produce one distinct sound together.

At this point, you will need to explain to the children that each finger represents one written letter, but because some sounds require more than one letter, those fingers in the map will be bundled close together.

In *figure 6*, you will find the map for any four letter word ending in a vowel team.

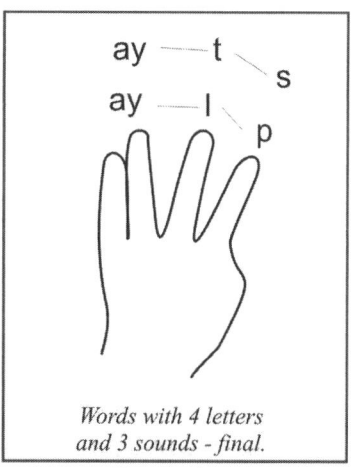

Words with 4 letters and 3 sounds - final.

Figure 6

If the vowel team is found inside the word (such as rain or goat), the finger map would vary slightly as shown in *figure 7*.

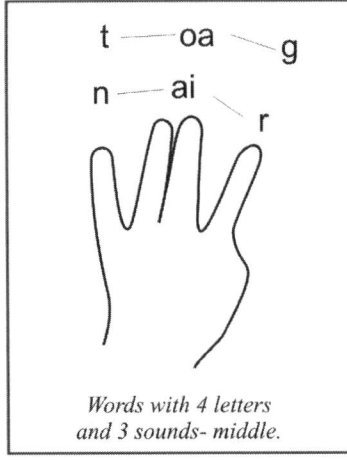

Words with 4 letters and 3 sounds- middle.

Figure 7

4. Digraphs are taught similarly to how we teach vowel teams. Tell the students that sometimes letters forget their normal sounds when they get near other letters, and then together the letters form a totally different sound.

For instance, display the letters S, T, H, C, W, and P. You can show the children that when you put /h/ next to/s/, the letters do not say /s/ /h/ anymore, but rather they lose their heads and say /sh/ when together. The same goes for putting /h/ next to any of the remaining displayed letters!

Drive this lesson home by assigning a sound to each student. One is S, one T, one H, etc. I then have them role play how sounds combine and "get silly" and forget the sounds they are supposed to make. First I have S walk back and forth saying her sound, "ssss". Then I have H join her and as they go back and forth, they now say, "shhh". I repeat this with the other letters: T and H saying TH as in "thin", C and H saying CH as in "chip", W and H saying WH as in "what", and finally P and H saying fff as in "phone."

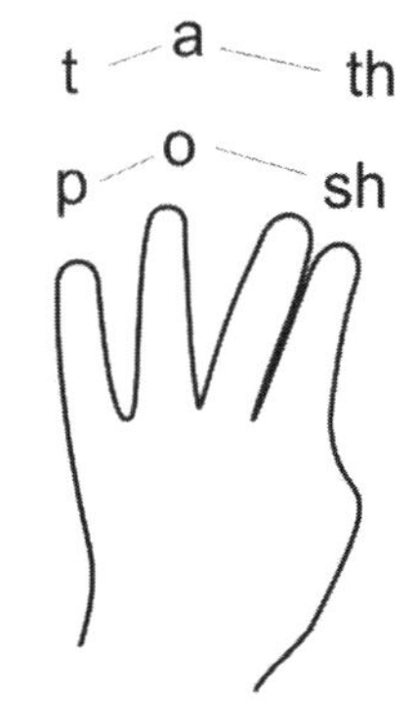

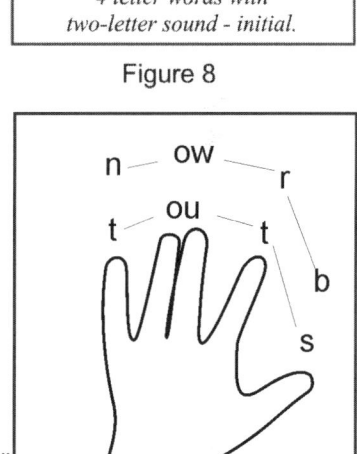

4 letter words with two-letter sound - initial.

Figure 8

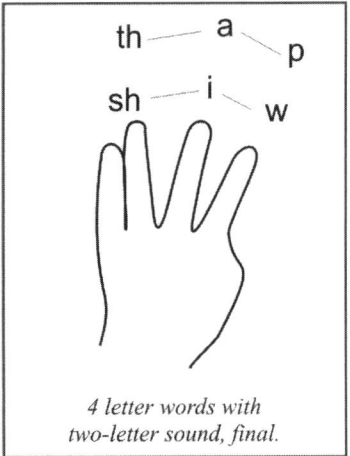

4 letter words with two-letter sound, final.

Figure 9

5. Diphthongs are presented the same way. These include "ou", "oi", "ow", "oy".

Figures 8 and following illustrate fingermapping for various types of words:

• <u>Initial digraph or diphthong</u> – *figure 8*. Examples of words include "**sh**ip, **sh**op, **th**at, **ch**op, **ch**ip, **ou**rs," and any other four letter words with an initial two letter sound.

• <u>Final digraph or diphthong</u> – *figure 9*. Examples of words would include "wi**sh**, di**sh**, ca**sh**, la**sh**, sl**ow**, st**ew**, pa**th**," and any other word with a final two letter sound.

• <u>Middle digraph or diphthong</u> – *figure 10*. Examples of words are myriad: "br**ow**n, cl**ow**n, cl**ou**d, st**ou**t," etc.

5 letter words with mid word 2 letter sound.

Figure 10

6. Fingermapping Letter Clusters

Wherever the letter cluster appears in the word, that is where the fingers will also cluster that represent each sound.

For example:
- eigh-t   (2 sounds, 5 letters), first 4 fingers together, 5th finger separate.
- sh-ou-t   (3 sounds, 5 letters), fingers 1-2 and 3-4 grouped, 5th finger separate.
- r-u-nn-er   (4 sounds, 6 letters), fingers 1 and 2 separate, 3-4 together and 5-6 together.
- f-a-th-er   (4 sounds, 6 letters), see figure 11.
- t-augh-t   (3 sounds, 6 letters), first finger separate, fingers 2-5 together, thumb of other hand for final t.

xi

When you need more than five fingers to spell a word, simply bring fingers from your right hand, starting with finger #1, which is your thumb. See example for "father" in *figure 11*.

Specific fingermapping guidelines will be presented in each lesson if any tricky situation should present itself.

The question has been asked whether or not the students should fingermap. I have never asked the children to fingermap because the power for them in fingermapping is totally visual. To ask them to fingermap will simply present them with an unnecessary skill to learn at a time when the simpler a lesson can be for them, the better!

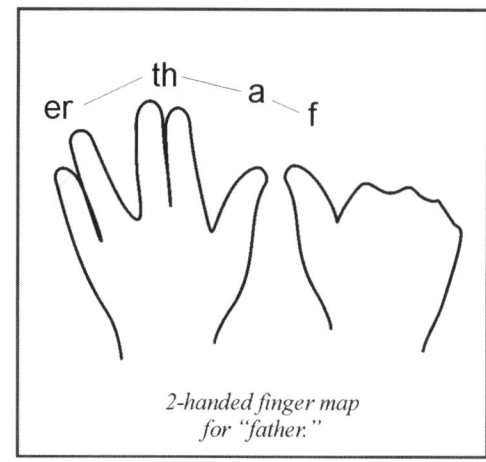

2-handed finger map for "father."

Figure 11

7. Fingermapping Silent E

Fingermapping Pinchy E: long vowel and silent final E.

Figure 12

Silent E can be very tricky for students who struggle with reading. We teach children to sound out words and they grind to a halt in the face of undecodable sound spellings and "silent" letters. In the case of the final, silent E, explain that the E is teaming up with other letters. In the case of long vowel spellings, the E is silent, but busy pinching the preceding vowel.

Notice in figure 12 that the example word "tame" has four letters, but we can only hear three. 4 letters = 4 fingers. But the E at the end makes no sound. He is busy pinching the A to make it say its name.

Examples of words with final, silent pinchy E:
• tame, lame, came, game, ate, etc. - page 14
• Eve, Pete, these - page 16
• five, live, white, mice, while, etc. - page 19

Examples of words with a final silent E when it is NOT a pinchy E: (fig. 13)
• live, give - page 11
• some, come, shove, above, dove, love - page 40
• please, grease - page 51. E is not pinching. The vowels are long vowel teams.
• whittle, whistle - page 79
• gaggle, wiggle, struggle - page 91
• simple, little, purple, people, sample, maple, apple - page 66
• whistle, bustle, rustle, castle - page 120
• pause, browse, lose, tease, cruise, freeze, snooze - page 97

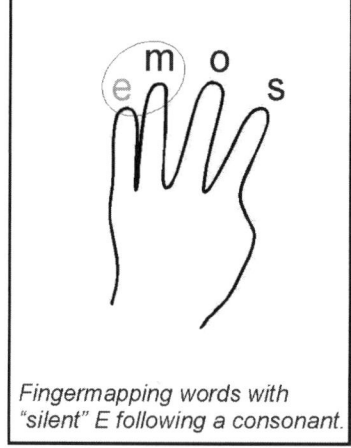

Fingermapping words with "silent" E following a consonant.

Figure 13

8. Fingermapping Multiple Syllable Words

When you get to **very long words**, what works best is to fingermap each syllable separately. Example: neigh-bor-hood, ad-ven-ture, fur-ni-ture, de-men-tia, par-ti-ci-pant, em-ploy-ment, un-for-tu-nate. This way you don't run out of fingers and the children can see that big words can be easily broken into manageable chunks. Have children separate words into syllables by drawing slash marks between them.

Fingermapping ING: show three fingers together to represent that word chunk either as one syllable (r-ing) or as a multi-syllable word (tap-ing). In this book the sound spelling is actually NG to accommodate all spellings: ang, ing, ung, ong, etc.

For compound words, fingermap each word separately. Example: under-stood. Or better yet, you can map by syllables: un-der-stood.

xii

DAILY ROUTINE

Preparation
Make enough copies of the lesson to give each child their own copy - and one for the teacher.
Give each child a yellow highlighter or crayon to use for coloring the sound spelling.
Each child will also need a whiteboard and a dry erase marker.

Day 1

- Pass out the lesson and highlighter.
- Identify the target sound for the lesson. Ex: on page 19, the target sound is Long I.
- Have children color only those letters which combine to make the target sound. You will find those sound spellings at the top, center of each lesson. The sound spellings on page 19 are **ie**, **i-e**.
- Draw attention to the fact that the letters that are left not colored can easily be sounded out.
- Using whiteboards and markers, play Quick Draw. If you have a classroom whiteboard, let the kids stand at the board. Otherwise, they can use individual whiteboards.

HOW TO PLAY QUICK DRAW:
- Say the first word while the children listen.
- Hold up fingers to show the structure of the word. One finger for each letter. If two or more letters combine to make a sound, those fingers will be close together. (Refer to instructions for fingermapping.)
- As you point to each finger, sound out the word, making sure the children are watching and sounding with you. One sound per finger or group of fingers.
- Say, "Sound and write." The children need to each say the sounds in the word as they write. Many will try to just go straight to writing, but it is important for them to orally sound, as this will guide them into correctly writing the word. If your child struggles with writing, let them use pull-down letters to form the words as they sound out the word.
- Do a quick visual check for errors. If there is a mistake, do the fingermapping again, asking the child to sound with you to discover where the error is.

Day 2

- Ask the children to tell you the target sound.
- Review the sentences containing their words.
- Play Quick Draw with the words. You may include other words with the same sound spelling as you feel the children are comfortable.

Day 3

- Review the sound and its spellings quickly.
- Review the sentences.
- Do a pretest with the words in order to find out where trouble spots might be.
- Use fingermapping as needed.

Day 4

- Play Quick Draw. This time include other words that follow the sound spelling in the lesson if desired.
- If the children are ready, go ahead and do the assessment.
- Give the children the opportunity to review and retake if they don't make 100%. As time goes by, you will find the children will learn their list of words very quickly and you might be able to go to only 3 sessions a week.

Child1st - Sounds, Sound Spellings, and Their Keywords*

Short Vowels:		Long Vowels:		Short ŏŏ		zh		/M/ Spellings	
a	at	a-e	ate	oo	book	s	measure	m	my
au	laugh	ai	rain	oul	could	si	television	mm	summer
		ay	day	u	put			mb	lamb
		ey	they			/ng/ /ngk/		mn	autumn
e	red	ea	break	Bossy R		nk	wink		
ea	head	eigh	eight	/er/		ng	king	/N/ Spellings	
ai	said	ei	rein	ur	turn			n	not
ie	friend	aigh	straight	ir	girl	/F/ Spellings		nn	dinner
				or	worm	f	fun	kn	know
i	it	e	he	er	her	ph	phone	gn	gnat
y	myth	ea	eat	ear	learn	gh	tough	pn	pneumonia
ai	certain	eo	people	yr	syrup	ff	off		
ui	build	e-e	Pete	ar	dollar			/R/ Spellings	
		ey	key	our	tourist	/G/ Spellings		r	ran
o	on	ee	see	/ar/		g	got	rr	arrow
a	want	ie	chief	ar	star	gh	ghost	wr	wren
aw	saw	i-e	petite	ear	heart	gg	baggy	rh	rhino
au	haul	i	Maria	uar	guard			re	here
al	walk	ei	ceiling	/or/		/H/ Spellings			
ou	cough	y	funny	or	for	h	hot	/S/ Spellings	
ough	bought			ore	more	wh	who	s	sit
augh	caught	i	find	ar	warm			ss	glass
		ie	pie	our	your	/J/ Spellings		c(e)	cent
u	up	i-e	like	oor	door	j	jam	st	whistle
o	other	igh	high	/air/		ge	large, gel	sc	scent
ou	rough	eigh	height	ar	vary	dge	fudge	se	horse
o-e	come	y	my	air	pair	g(y)	gym	ce	lace
oe	does	eye	eye	ear	pear	g(i)	giant	c(y)	cyclops
oo	flood	is	island	are	care			c(i)	city
		ais	aisle	ere	where	/K/ /KW/ Spellings			
Sounds of Y				eir	their	k	kiss	/T/ Spellings	
y	my	o	go	uar	guarantee	c	cat	t	tap
y	funny	ow	snow	/ear/		ck	kick	tt	matter
y	myth	oa	goat	eer	deer	ch	Chris	bt	doubt
		o-e	home	ier	pier	qu	queen	pt	pterodactyl
Diphthongs:		oe	Joe	ere	here			ed	passed
oi	join	ough	though	ear	near				
oy	joy	oo	poor	Digraphs		/L/ Spellings		/Z/ Spellings	
		ou	your	sh	she	l	left	z	zoo
ow	cow	u-e	use	s	sure	ll	well	zz	fizz
ou	out	ue	cue	ch	machine	el	parcel	s	his
ough	drought	u	pupil	ss	assure	le	little	se	lose
		ew	few	ci	special	il	fossil	ze	snooze
Sounds of 'ough'		Long ōō		ce	ocean	al	rural	x	xylophone
ough	though	oo	cool	ch	child				
ough	tough	ew	new	tch	catch				
ough	through	o-e	lose						
ough	thought	u-e	flute	th	the				
ough	bough	ue	blue	th	with				
ough	cough	ui	suit	wh	when				
		ou	you						
		oe	shoe						
		o	to						
		ough	through						
		u	flu						

*W, V, P, B, D not included. ©2005 Sarah Major www.child1st.com

USING KEYWORDS EFFECTIVELY

If you refer to the chart on the previous page, "Sounds, Sound Spellings, and Their Keywords," you'll find that we have identified and grouped the sound spellings together by sound. Each sound spelling has a related keyword. For example, in the box for the sound oo, there are three sound spellings: OO as in "book," OUL as in "could," and U as in "put."

We chose the smallest words we could for keywords in order to accommodate beginners. However, having identified a keyword, it will be simple to group far more complex words around each keyword.

In my kindergarten classroom, each time we learned a sound spelling, we'd write the keyword at the top of a long strip of paper, then post it on the wall. As children came across words containing that sound spelling, they wrote them on the strip. In a kindergarten classroom, the list of words might look like this at first: "star," "far," "car," "part," "art," "tar." Then over time, words can be added: "smart," "park," "start," "party," "depart," "department," and so on.

If you are working with older students, you can use keywords to help them analyze longer words.

You teach sounds and their spellings,

Sound:	Sound:
/er/	/oo/
Sound Spellings:	Sound Spellings:
er, ir, or, ur, ear, yr, ar, our	oo, oul, u
Keywords:	Keywords:
her, girl, worm, turn, learn, syrup, dollar, tourist	book, could, put

the child encounters a new word,

and uses known words to analyze it.
her   book

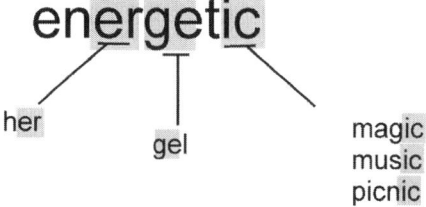

her   gel   magic
              music
              picnic

Even in a long word, once sound spellings are highlighted, what is left are letters that are easy to decode.

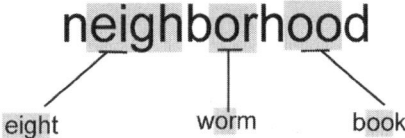

eight   worm   book

The more you focus on sound spellings and analyzing new words with your students, the more fluent your students will become at identifying those spelling patterns and using them to figure out new words. This practice is especially valuable for dominant right-brained learners! There is nothing more effective for improving reading ability than understanding how to spell sounds.

Sound Spelling Tracking Sheet

Name_____

Use this form to keep track of progress throughout the book. If your student skipped early lessons, just check off the lessons skipped. You will need one sheet printed front/back for each student.

PG	DATE	SKILL / NOTES	✓	PG	DATE	SKILL / NOTES	✓
1	/	Short A, Level 1		36	/	/K/, Level 1	
2	/	Short E, Level 1		37	/	/K/ & /KW/, Level 2	
3	/	Short I, Level 1		38	/	Short E, Level 3	
4	/	Short O, Level 1		39	/	Short O, Level 3	
5	/	Short U, Level 1		40	/	Short U, Level 2	
6	/	Short A, Level 2		41	/	/AIR/, Level 1	
7	/	Digraph SH, Level 1		42	/	/EAR/, Level 1	
8	/	Digraph TH, Level 1		43	/	/EAR/, Level 2	
9	/	Digraph CH, Level 1		44	/	/OR/, Level 1	
10	/	Short E, Level 2		45	/	/OR/, Level 2	
11	/	Short I, Level 2		46	/	Soft C & G, Level 1	
12	/	NG & NK, Level 1		47	/	Soft C & G, Level 2	
13	/	Short O, Level 2		48	/	Double Consonants, Level 1	
14	/	Long A, Level 1		49	/	Double Consonants, Level 2	
15	/	Long A, Level 2		50	/	Long E, Level 2	
16	/	Long E, Level 1		51	/	Long E, Level 3	
17	/	Final Y /Long I/ & /Long E/, Level 1		52	/	Long O, Level 4	
18	/	Long I, Level 1		53	/	Digraph TH, Level 2	
19	/	Long I, Level 2		54	/	Digraph CH, Level 2	
20	/	Long I, Level 3		55	/	Digraph WH, Level 1	
21	/	Long I, Level 4		56	/	ŌŌ, Level 3	
22	/	/L/, Level 1		57	/	ŎŎ, Level 2	
23	/	Long O, Level 1		58	/	/OI/, Level 2	
24	/	Long O, Level 2		59	/	/OW/, Level 2	
25	/	Long O, Level 3		60	/	Schwa /UH/	
26	/	Long U		61	/	NG & NK, Level 2	
27	/	ŌŌ, Level 1		62	/	Final Y /Long E/, Level 2	
28	/	ŌŌ, Level 2		63	/	/ER/, Level 3	
29	/	ŎŎ, Level 1		64	/	/OR/, Level 3	
30	/	/OI/, Level 1		65	/	/F/, Level 1	
31	/	/OW/, Level 1		66	/	/L/, Level 2	
32	/	/ER/, Level 1		67	/	/R/, Level 1	
33	/	/ER/, Level 2		68	/	Past Tense, /T/, /D/, /ED/, Level 1	
34	/	/AR/, Level 1		69	/	Past Tense, /T/, /D/, /ED/, Level 2	
35	/	/AR/, Level 2		70	/	Plurals, +S, +ES, Level 1	

Child1st Publications LLC | child1st.com | 800-881-0912

Name_____

PG	DATE	SKILL / NOTES	✓
71	/	Short O, Level 4	
72	/	Short U, Level 3	
73	/	Long A, Level 3	
74	/	Long A, Level 4	
75	/	Homophones, Level 1	
76	/	Homophones, Level 2	
77	/	Long E, Level 4	
78	/	Long E, Level 5	
79	/	Digraph WH, Level 2	
80	/	/OW/, Level 3	
81	/	/OW/, Level 4	
82	/	/ER/, Level 4	
83	/	/ER/, Level 5	
84	/	/AR/, Level 3	
85	/	/AIR/, Level 2	
86	/	/AIR/, Level 3	
87	/	/OR/, Level 4	
88	/	Soft C & G, Level 3	
89	/	Soft C & G, Level 4	
90	/	/F/, Level 2	
91	/	/G/	
92	/	/L/, Level 3	
93	/	/L/, Level 4	
94	/	/M/	
95	/	/N/	
96	/	/T/, Level 1	
97	/	/Z/	
98	/	OUGH, Level 1	
99	/	OUGH, Level 2	
100	/	Past Tense, /T/, /D/, /ED/, Level 3	
101	/	Plurals, +IES, +S, +ES, Level 2	
102	/	Special Endings, +N and +EN	
103	/	Special Endings, +ISH, +IST, +IZE	
104	/	Special Endings, +SURE, +TURE	
105	/	Special Endings, +CIA, +TIA, +SIA	

PG	DATE	SKILL / NOTES	✓
106	/	Homophones, Level 3	
107	/	Short I, Level 3	
108	/	Digraph SH, Level 2	
109	/	Digraph SH, Level 3	
110	/	ŌŌ, Level 4	
111	/	ŌŌ, Level 5	
112	/	/OI/, Level 3	
113	/	/OI/, Level 4	
114	/	Double Consonants, Level 3	
115	/	Double Consonants, Level 4	
116	/	/F/, Level 3	
117	/	/F/, Level 4	
118	/	/R/, Level 2	
119	/	/R/, Level 3	
120	/	/S/, Level 1	
121	/	/S/, Level 2	
122	/	/T/, Level 2	
123	/	Plurals, Level 3	
124	/	Plurals, Level 4	
125	/	Special Endings, +ER	
126	/	Special Endings, +OR	
127	/	Special Endings, +ION, +IAN	
128	/	Special Endings, +SION, +TION, +CIAN	
129	/	Special Endings, +MENT, +ATE, +NESS	
130	/	Special Endings, +ANT	
131	/	Special Endings, +ENT, +EER	
132	/	Special Endings, +ITY, +TY	
133	/	Special Endings, +ARY	
134	/	Special Endings, +ALLY, +LY, +WARD	
135	/	Special Endings, +OUS	
136	/	Special Endings, +CIOUS, +SCIOUS, +TIOUS	
137	/	Special Endings, +IOUS	
138	/	Special Endings, +EOUS, +UOUS	

Notes:

TEACHING NOTES

Follow this Lesson Sequence. Use Teaching Notes to prepare teacher's copy before teaching lesson.
Follow "Daily Routine" p. xiii.

PAGE	CONTENT	NOTES - see fingermapping notes at the bottom of the page on each lesson.
1	Short A	Page ix, Section 1. All words are made of single letter sounds which are easily heard. Follow the Lesson Sequence for every lesson. See pages ix-x: "When you present the lesson for the first time..."
2	Short E	All words are made of single letter sounds. Say each sound and write a letter as you say each sound.
3	Short I	All words are made of single letter sounds. See notes Lesson 1.
4	Short O	Single letter sounds except "OFF." Underline FF. 2 letters, 1 sound. **From now on**, each time you find a sound needs more than one letter, underline them on your teacher's copy.
5	Short U	All words are made of single letter sounds. Sound and write all individual sounds.
6	Short A	Single letter sounds except for "L AU GH." AU=short A. GH=/F/. Underline AU and GH. This will be covered again on page 65.
7	/SH/ (Sounds like SH)	Highlight all SH and CE (in OCEAN). From now on, underline all multiple letter sounds.
8	/TH/ (Sounds like TH)	Highlight TH's. Underline EY in THEY.
9	/CH/ (Sounds like CH)	Highlight CH. Underline EA in EACH, OW in CHOW, LL in CHILL. 2 letters, one sound. Note that EACH has only two sounds: E and CH. CHOW also just has two sounds: CH and OW.
10	Short E	All words are made of single letter sounds except for LL in 4 words. Underline LL.
11	Short I	Underline 2 letter sounds: LL, TH, SH, CK, VE (see pg. xii, Fig. 13 for "silent" final E).
12	NG & NK	Highlight target sounds: NG and NK. Sound and write all other (individual) sounds.
13	Short O	Underline SS, NG, AL, CH. All other sounds are 1-letter sounds. See note on lesson re: AL spelling.
14	Long A	See page xii, Fig. 12. Pinchy E is silent but pinches the vowel to make it long. So he has a finger when mapping the word, but his lips are pinched shut. Draw a little curve under the word, from Pinchy E to the vowel he is pinching, to show they are connected.
15	Long A	Underline TH. Highlight target spellings. All other sounds are 1-letter sounds.
16	Long E	See page xii, Fig. 12. Pinchy E for EVEN, EVE, PETE, THESE. Draw curves for Pinchy E to vowels he is pinching. Underline TH.
17	Sounds of Y	Underline double letters and CH. Sound and write all other individual sounds.
18	Long I	Underline CH, WH. Sound and write all other individual sounds.
19	Long I	Pinchy E rule, pg. xii, Fig. 12. Draw curves for Pinchy E. Underline WH.
20	Long I	Highlight target spellings (IGH). Sounds require 3 letters/fingers.
21	Long I	Highlight target spellings (EIGH, IS, AIS, EYE). Sounds require 2-4 letters/fingers.
22	/L/ /Sounds like L/	Underline IE in LIE. PUPIL is only IL word: (where IL sounds like L).
23	Long O	Underline TH. All other words are made of single letter sounds.
24	Long O	Curve for Pinchy E. Note: in blends such as STR, all sounds are heard, so have the students say each sound as they are sounding and writing. There is no need to teach blends as it just makes more for children to memorize - something visual learners don't do well.
25	Long O	Underline SH, KN, TH. Highlight target sounds which are 2-letter sounds.
26	Long U	Highlight. Underline IL in PUPIL. UNITE, USE, FUSE, MULE are Pinchy E words. Draw curves for them.
27	/OO/ as in "cool"	Underline WH in WHOM /H/. Underline AY, TH, ER. SUPER, FLUTE are Pinchy E words.
28	/OO/ as in "cool"	Underline TH, SH, LL, WH (/H/), ED in MOVED /D/.
29	/OO/ as in "book"	Underline LL, SH.
30	/OI/	Highlight the target sounds from the top of the page. There are no multiple letter sounds to underline.
31	/OW/	Underline SE in HOUSE. See page xii, Fig. 13.
32	/ER/	Underline ERE in WERE and VE in SERVE.

Page	CONTENT	NOTES - see fingermapping notes at the bottom of the page on each lesson.
33	/ER/	Underline TH, SH, CH, NG.
34	/AR/	No special notes. Follow lesson sequence.
35	/AR/	Underline CH and GE in CHARGE, and GE in LARGE. Slash to separate syllables in M-AR / K-E-T, S-C-AR / L-E-T.
36	/K/	Underline LE in TACKLE, SS in KISS. Pinchy E words: PIKE, BIKE, CAKE, CAVE, KITE.
37	/K/ & /QU/	Underline EE, AR, ZE, OO. QU starts out sounding like K, but ends up sounding like KW.
38	Short E	Underline ER in sweater. Slashes between syllables - map syllables separately. Page xii, Section 8.
39	Short O	Underline TH, ER, WH, TCH, SH.
40	Short U	Underline ER, TH, SH and consonant+E pairs at bottom of page. See Fig. 13, page xii.
41	/AIR/ R Controlled	Underline WH, TH, CH. See hint for THEIR at bottom of lesson.
42	/EAR/ R Controlled	Underline SH, CH
43	/EAR/ R Controlled	Underline ED in PIERCED where ED sounds like /T/.
44	/OR/ R Controlled	Underline OI and SE separately in TORTOISE. OI /i/ and SE /S/.
45	/OR/	Underline CH, ER, TH, NG. You may separate HORNET, FORGET, and MORNING into syllables and map each syllable separately. Draw curves for Pinchy E on TORE, WORE, BEFORE, SCORE, MORE.
46	C /S/ & G /J/	In column 1, CE is a sound spelling that sounds like S, but the E also is a Pinchy E, reaching back to the A to make it say its name. In column 2, G sounds like J when followed by E, I, and Y at the beginning of words, but also GE sounds like J when at the end of a word, such as LARGE. Underline LE, IE, FFE.
47	C /S/ & G /J/	In column 1, CE sounds like S at the ends of words. Those endings will require 2 letters to spell the S sound. In the words where C is followed by an I, only the C will be highlighted as the I's that follow either are R Controlled (IR) or they make their own sound (ex: CITY). In column 2, GE and DGE sound like a J.
48	Double Consonant	Underline double consonants and ER. Students can make a slash mark between syllables, dividing each word between matching consonants.
49	Double Consonant	Underline double consonants, ED /D/ (GRINNED, CARED, SMILED) and ED /T/ (TAPPED, WRAPPED, FIXED), WR, and NG. FIX breaks the rule with its short vowel and only one consonant.
50	Long E	Underline SH, WH, CH, SE (in CHEESE), NN in FUNNY.
51	Long E	Underline SE in PLEASE and GREASE, LL in REALLY, VE in LEAVE, and WH in WHEAT.
52	Long O	Underline TH. See also page 64 for OU spelling that is R Controlled as in YOUR.
53	/TH/	Draw curves for Pinchy E words. Underline EE, ER, SE, CK, NG, NK, EIR, ERE. Note that TOGETHER is easy to learn to spell if you separate into 3 little words: TO GET HER. "We will get her together."
54	/CH/	Underline TH in THATCH.
55	/WH/	Underline ERE, CH, EE, and ED /D/. Curve for Pinchy E in WHALE.
56	/OO/ as in "cool"	Underline SE in BRUISE, TH in THROUGH.
57	/OO/ as in "book"	Underline SH, SS, ED /T/ in LOOKED. Slashes for syllables.
58	/OI/	Underline SE in NOISE, CE in VOICE, ER.
59	/OW/	Underline ER, TH, SH, SE in MOUSE, Pinchy E in OUTSIDE. Slash syllables.
60	Schwa /UH/	Underline vowel teams EE, OU, AI, AY, EA, and VE ending in ABOVE. 3 Pinchy E curves. AWHILE, ALIVE, AWAKE.
61	NG & /NGK/	Underline OR and TH.
62	Y /Long E/	Underline double consonants, ER, CH, CK, and QU.
63	/ER/	Underline EY in TURKEY, AR in ARMOR, SE in WORSE, and TH.
64	/OR/	Underline TH, SE, GE. Teach "OUR" words depending on your pronunciation of TOURIST.
65	/F/	Three Pinchy E words in column 1. Underline OU and AU spellings. AU - short A. OU - short O p. 71, short U p. 72.
66	/L/	Draw slashes to separate syllables in long words. Underline double consonants. Underline R Controlled pairs: UR, ER, OR. EO, OY.
67	/R/	Draw slashes to separate syllables. Underline TH, ME in RHYME, and NG in WRONG. 3 Pinchy E words RHODE, WRITE, WROTE. Draw curves for Pinchy E.
68	Past Tense	Underline double consonants. Underline AY and AR, EE, AI in column 2. You can hear both sounds in the -ED ending starting with WANTED and ending with WAITED. 2 sounds = 2 fingers when fingermapping.

Page	CONTENT	NOTES - see fingermapping notes at the bottom of the page on each lesson.
69	Past Tense	Underline double consonants and CK, CH, WR, EA, OR, OW, OA. From HEADED to TREATED, you can hear both sounds in the final -ED. Two sounds and two fingers.
70	Plurals S, ES	Underline double consonants, R Controlled (IR, ER, AR), Diphthong OY, and vowel teams EA, OA. Underline CK. Digraph SH. The sound of S in the first column is like Z. In the second column, you can hear both sounds in the final -ES. Two sounds = two fingers.
71	Short O	Underline TH, GH /F/ in COUGH, MN /M/ in AUTUMN, ER, SE in BECAUSE.
72	Short U	Underline GH /F/, CH, NG, and ER. Use slashes to separate syllables.
73	Long A	Slash syllables. Underline SH, FF, CH. Note: AY spelling is mostly found at the end of a word or a syllable. Ex: AW<u>AY</u> is at end of word while P<u>AY</u>|MENT has AY at end of syllable.
74	Long A	Underline OR and GN in REIGN.
75	Homophones	Underline vowel teams AY, EIGH, EA, AI and draw curves for Pinchy E spellings. Underline LL in SELL and CELL.
76	Homophones	Underline R Controlled spellings: ERE, EAR, ERE, EIR. Underline KN, OU, SC.
77	Long E	Underline TH, CH, SH, NG. Underline consonant+E endings -CE, -VE, -ZE, -NE.
78	Long E	Underline ZE in SEIZE and -SURE (see page 104). For EIR in WEIRD, see also the R Controlled spelling lesson on page 43. Underline NG, -VE, -PT, -TE, -LE.
79	/WH/	Underline ER, OO, TT, LE, ST /S/, CK, IR, SH. Draw curves for Pinchy E words: WHILE, WHITE.
80	/OW/	Draw slashes for syllables. Underline AI, CH, TH, ER, -CE endings.
81	/OW/	Draw slashes for syllables. Underline LL, ER, -CE endings, CH, AR.
82	/ER/	Underline VE, CE, SE, GE. Underline CH, TH, RR, EW, AI. Use slashes for syllables. "OUR" words included depending on your pronunciation of TOURIST. Or see page 64 for /OR/.
83	/ER/	Use slashes to separate words into syllables. Underline double consonants, QU, VE ending. Draw curves to show Pinchy E for PURFUME and CIRCULATE.
84	/AR/	Underline UE in ARGUE, LE, TH, ER, CH, NG. Note that UAR /AR/ in GUARD is a 3-letter sound spelling. Any word that has "guard" in it will share that spelling. For example: guardian, lifeguard, etc. Draw slashes to show syllables.
85	/AIR/	Draw slashes to separate syllables. Underline SH, EE.
86	/AIR/	Draw slashes to separate syllables.
87	/OR/	Slashes for syllables. Underline AU, TH, ERE, AR, CE, ER, OUS, RR. Curve for Pinchy E.
88	C /S/ & G /J/	Underline EI, AR, ER, UR. Use slashes for syllables.
89	C /S/ & G /J/	Underline OUR, GG, & double consonants. Note that in column 1, you will highlight -CE endings and G /J/ at the beginnings of words. In column 2, highlight -GE endings.
90	/F/	Use slashes for syllables. Underline -ED /D/ endings, ER, OR, IR, double consonants.
91	/G/	Underline OU /OO/, TT, -ER, EE, -LE, IR, EA, OA, NG, double consonants.
92	/L/	Use slashes for syllables. Underline OU, AR, SS, OU.
93	/L/	Use slashes for syllables. Map syllables separately. Underline TION in R<u>ATION</u>AL - see page 128. Example: N<u>ATION</u>. Underline IS /I/, AIS /I/, and TT.
94	/M/	Underline OW, AU, TH, ER.
95	/N/	Use slashes for syllables. Underline EW, CK, EE, CK, ER, AW, KN. Two Pinchy E words - GNOME and KNIFE.
96	/T/	Underline double consonants, OO, NG, -VE, -CE, ER.
97	/Z/	Slashes for syllables. Underline PH, AU, OW, EA, UI, EE, OO, SS, OR. Pinchy E on XYLOPHONE, PHASE, ARISE, AMAZE.
98	Sounds of OUGH	Fingermapping for first column is C-OU-GH, T-R-OU-GH, R-OU-GH, T-OU-GH, E-N-OU-GH, S-L-OU-GH. Second column: TH-OUGH. A-L-TH-OUGH. Underline OU, GH, OUGH, TH.
99	Sounds of OUGH	Underline TH. In this lesson, the OUGH is mapped as one sound in all the words. TH-R-OUGH, B-OUGH, S-L-OUGH, etc.
100	Past Tense	Separate syllables with slashes. Underline sounds with multiple letters such as AI, ER, and double consonants. In column 1, ED has one sound /D/. In column 2, there are two distinct sounds: E and D. Underline OR, OI, ER, and double consonants.
101	Plurals IES, S	Use slashes to separate syllables. Underline AR, OR, PP, ER, EA, OU, CH, AY, IE, DG, LL, EY, OA. The -ES endings on WOLVES, LOAVES, HALVES are one sound, but two letters. The AL in HALVES is one sound unless you are used to pronouncing the L in that word.

xx

Page	CONTENT	NOTES - see fingermapping notes at the bottom of the page on each lesson.
102	Ends N, EN	Slashes for syllables. Underline IGH, AIGH, OR, and double consonants. In column 1, the root words end in an E already so you only add an N and you can hear both the E and the N in those words. In column 2, FRIGHTEN and STRAIGHTEN add an EN, but the bottom two words require the doubling of the T so the E in EN won't pinch the vowel and make it long.
103	Ends ISH, IST, IZE	Use slashes for separating syllables. Underline CH, OO, SC, AR, OUR, OR, CI, AR, ER.
104	Ends SURE, TURE	Use slashes. Underline vowel teams in column 1. Apart from those, these longer words are super easy to sound and write when done a syllable at a time.
105	Ends CIA, TIA, SIA	Underline AR, OR, ER, EE. Use slashes to separate syllables.
106	Homophones	Use slashes. Underline all multi-letter sounds. LE, AI, EIGH, OA, SE, OUR, EI, ER.
107	Short I	Use slashes. Underline ER, SH, OU, RH, TH.
108	/SH/	Use slashes. Underline URE, AR, OR, OU, OE, OW, LL, EAR, NG.
109	/SH/	Underline URE, UE, ION, -NE. IOUS is a special ending taught on page 136.
110	/OO/ as in "cool"	Slashes. Underline TH, LE, EA.
111	/OO/ as in "cool"	Slashes. Underline TH, -VE, -NE, PP.
112	/OI/	The words in this lesson are long but not hard. Use slashes to break them up first. Underline double consonants. Underline GE ending, ER, ED /D/, TURE, NG.
113	/OI/	Underline OUS /us/, PP, CH, NG, ER, URE, -CE.
114	Double Consonant	Slashes for syllables. Underline double letters. Underline IR, OR, ER, OU, -LE, -CE, ED /D/
115	Double Consonant	Slashes for syllables. Underline -VE, AU, AL in APPROVAL, TION, CE. Note Pinchy E words and draw curves.
116	/F/	Slashes. Underline AR, EA, OE.
117	/F/	Slashes. Underline CIAN /shun/. AR, -ES, OR, ORE.
118	/R/	Use slashes for the longer words. Underline EU in RHEUMATISM /Long U/. Underline LE ending on two words, TH, OR, NG, NK, and ER ending. In the first column, we encounter Pinchy Vowels other than E. In RHYNE and RHIZOMES, there is a Pinchy E. In RHESUS, the U is pinching the E. In RHAPSODY, the final Y acts as a vowel and pinches the O. Make sure students understand what the words mean in this lesson. RHYNE is a river, RHESUS is a monkey, RHEUMATISM is pain in joints and or muscles, while RHIZOMES are shoots sent out underground in order to form a new plant nearby. RHETORIC refers to effective persuasive speaking, RHAPSODY refers to music that expresses a lot of emotion. WRANGLE = argue, WRATH = anger.
119	/R/	Slashes for syllables. Underline AR in RHUBARB, IGH in WRIGHT, NG and ER in WRANGLER, CH, TCH, and CK in the next three words. AI and TH in WRAITH, ST and LE in WRESTLE, EA and TH in WREATH. A WRAITH is a ghost. Underline double consonants.
120	/S/	Slashes for syllables. Underline WH and LE in the first column. OR, CE, LL, AR in the second column. A BUSTLE was a poof of fabric under a skirt to make it stick out. It also means a lot of activity. Other words are defined at the bottom of the lesson.
121	/S/	Slashes for syllables. Highlight the target sound spellings first. Note that in GROCERY, the E performs two functions. It helps C be soft and it is also R Controlled ER. Underline OR, and ER (in CYLINDER). To CONCEAL means to hide.
122	/T/	Use slashes to separate syllables. Highlight target spellings. Note the word definitions at the bottom of the page. Underline LE and AI, NE in PTOMAINE.
123-124	Plural Suffixes	In these lessons, syllables are important to identify and map separately. Also watch for little words inside larger ones. After marking the syllables, note the small words and ask the students to underline them as desired. On p. 124, I see QUIT and TOES in MOSQUITOES. POT and TOES in POTATOES, etc. In this column also note the headings for each group of words. In the first group, all words end in O, and to make a plural you add ES. In the second group, the words end in F, and to make a plural you remove the F and add VES. At the bottom, the words end in Y, and you remove the Y and add IES. On p. 123 at the top, the reason the first word has an S ending is because they are plural. More than one passer, more than one mother, more than one father. At the bottom of the column, we have plurals as well, but the plural refers to the whole word. Underline multiple letter sounds.
125-126	Suffixes ER, OR	Definitely draw slashes for syllables. Locate and underline all multi-letter sounds such as double consonants, AY, OR, ER, SH, TCH, AR. The main focus of these lessons is to identify which words end in OR and which end in ER. In this situation, the sentences that group like words together and their illustrations will provide strong memory prompts. Encourage the students to read each lesson and study the illustrations. They also can over-pronounce the endings, OR and ER, when they say the words.

xxi

Page	CONTENT	NOTES - see fingermapping notes at the bottom of the page on each lesson.
127	Suffixes ION, IAN	Again, slashes for syllables. Focus on the difference between ION and IAN endings. Discuss each sentence and study its illustration so the students understand what is going on in each one. The "solution" in the first sentence is to move away from the snake. Poor guy having to cry through cutting up a million onions! The librarian probably wants the custodian to stop telling jokes and start cleaning! The electrician is guarding the musician from being interrupted while practicing. Underline AR in LIBRARIAN and UAR in GUARDIAN. For ION suffix, note the "eye on" picture at left. Underline doubles.
128	Suffixes SION, TION, CIAN	Syllables. Highlighting. Read sentences together and discuss what each one means. In the first sentence, there was a car which crashed and then sank in the water. Students can make up what might be going on. Which election? Election about what? Is it something that is being voted on that will affect plantations? For those space fans, sentence 3 might be interesting. The visual cue for CIAN is "See I Ann" - C-I-AN. ER, LL, SS
129	Suffixes MENT, ATE, NESS	Slashes for syllables. Highlight target spellings. In this lesson MENT as a suffix means the action of (the root word). For example AMUSEMENT is the action of being amused. ARGUMENT is the action of arguing, and so on. Note how the illustrations show the meaning of the words in the sentences. For the sake of expanding vocabulary and increasing comprehension, really take time to discuss each sentence/illustration until you are sure your students get it. Underline AR, OY, GE, CC, ER, RR, SS, OR, MM, LE, CK. Now go back and draw curves under the words to show Pinchy E. (E in AMUSEMENT, ARGUMENT. The endings of the last six words in the first column and the first three in column 2.)
130	Suffix ANT	Slashes for syllables. Again, focus on meaning and comprehension. It might help in the first sentence for the students to label the picture. Which figure is the tenant, which is the assistant, and which is the lieutenant? Underline ER, SS, TT, IEU, AR, EA, PP.
131	Suffixes ENT, EER	Slashes for syllables. Read the sentences together and have the students put them into their own words. "I'm sure the superintendant is against the current president because he wants to be elected himself." And "The engineer drives without pay because his real career is writing sonnets (poems of 14 lines, 10 syllables per line) and he writes better than any pioneer or mountain person." Underline double consonants, AR, OU, ER, EER.
132	Suffixes ITY, TY	Slashes. FEALTY means dedication to someone and LOYALTY is very similar. It means you are for someone and will always remain faithful to them...to have their back. The only sounds to underline are OY in LOYALTY and CI /sh/ in SPECIALTY. All the other sounds can be heard on their own.
133	Suffix ARY	Slashes for syllables. Pay attention to word and sentence meanings. In the last sentence, the guy in the closet is the backup for the main speaker - in case the main speaker doesn't show up. Underline double consonants, OR.
134	Suffixes ALLY, LY, WARD	Slashes and underline double consonants and TION, ARE, OO, SE, AR, CE, AI, OU, ER, EA. Identify Pinchy E and draw little curves. In column 1 at the top, look for the little words in the big words. IDEALLY has idea and ally. FINALLY has fin and ally. The suffix WARD means in that direction. In the direction of OUT or IN or UP, etc. LY suffix refers to how something was done. It's a word which tells us more about what is being done. CAREFULLY means done with care.
135	Suffix OUS	Slashes and underlining - AR, OR, ER, UR, OU, EA, RR, AI. Suffix OUS means "has, with, or full of." For example, HUMOROUS means with or full of humor. DANGEROUS means with or full of danger. Point out that OU is a sound spelling that appears frequently in our language. A reminder is to say, "OH, YOU!" These words are long but may be sounded out pretty easily when broken into syllables.
136	Suffixes CIOUS, SCIOUS, TIOUS, XIOUS	Slashes for syllables. Underline SC. In the first sentence, apparently the soup was pretty nasty and horrible. Note the flies buzzing around and the dead fish in the bowl! The person speaking in this sentence is pretty upset that the boy said it was delicious! With this suffix, use the phrase "I owe you" to help children remember the letter sequence.
137	Suffixes IOUS	Follow the same procedure as in the last few lessons. Focus on comprehension of the sentences. The words in this lesson are adjectives and the suffix means something like "full of." GLORIOUS means with or full of glory. CAUTIOUS means with or full of caution. Underline AR, UR, OR, AU, ER.
138	Suffix EOUS, UOUS	Follow the same procedure as in the last few lessons. CONGRUOUS means the cars fit together nicely, ARDUOUS means difficult, IMPETUOUS means rash, and AMBIGUOUS means not really clear. Underline OR, OUR, AR.

xxii

SHORT A
LEVEL 1

Name_____

Sound: /ă/
Keyword: at

Use a yellow highlighter to color the sound spelling for /ă/.

a /ă/

She has a cat who ran at my ham and sat.

I had to ask, "Can you scat?"

Fingermapping: Figures 3 & 4

© 2018 Sarah K Major

SHORT E
LEVEL 1

Name_____

Sound: /ĕ/
Keyword: red

Use a yellow highlighter to color the sound spelling for /ĕ/.

Fingermapping: Figure 3
© 2018 Sarah K Major

SHORT I
LEVEL 1

Name_____

Sound: /ĭ/
Keyword: it

Use a yellow highlighter to color the sound spelling for /ĭ/.

i /ĭ/

See
if
it
is
in
its
big
pen.

Did
his
six
trick **him?**

Fingermapping: Figure 3

© 2018 Sarah K Major

SHORT O
LEVEL 1

Sound: /ŏ/
Keyword: on

Name_____

Use a yellow highlighter to color the sound spelling for /ŏ/.

o /ŏ/

She **got**
on
and **off**
of
the slide.

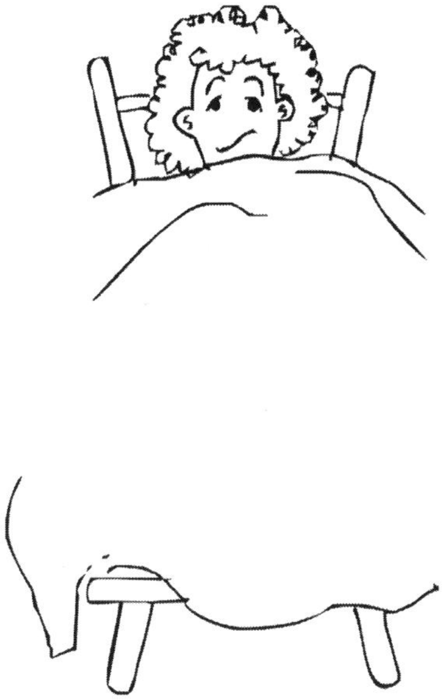

Dot
got
hot
in her **cot.**

It's to **Tom**
from **Mom!**

Fingermapping: Figure 3

© 2018 Sarah K Major

SHORT U
LEVEL 1

Name_____

Sound: /ŭ/
Keyword: up

Use a yellow highlighter to color the sound spelling for /ŭ/.

u /ŭ/

Come **up**
with **us**
and **run**
in the **sun!**

We **just**
must
dust.

If you **jump**
you'll **bump**
the **grump!**

Fingermapping: all words are one letter per finger.

SHORT A
LEVEL 2

Name_____

Sound: /ă/
Keyword: at

Use a yellow highlighter to color the sound spellings for /ă/.

a, au /ă/

In the **past**, I was **last**. Now I'm **fast**.

Fran will **plan** for a **clan**!

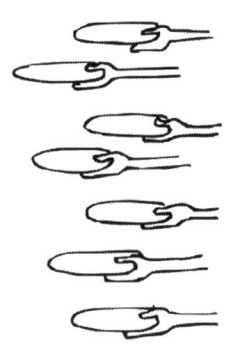

I **stand** in the **sand** to give the **grand band** a **hand**!

It's the best in the **land**!

He will **laugh** and **cough**!*

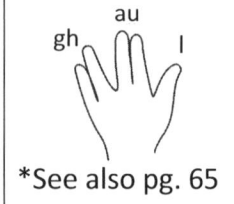

*See also pg. 65

Fingermapping: Figures 4 & 5

© 2018 Sarah K Major

DIGRAPH SH
LEVEL 1

Sound: /sh/
Keyword: she

Name_____

Use a yellow highlighter to color the sound spellings for /sh/.

sh, ce /sh/

She will shop in the ship on the ocean.

The ship is on the ocean.

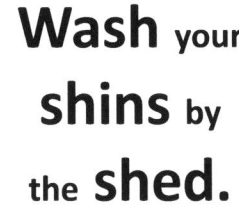

Wash your shins by the shed.

I wish the fish was a shad. It's a sham!

Fingermapping: Figure 6. SH, CE are one sound. Ex: w-a-sh, o-ce-a-n.

© 2018 Sarah K Major

DIGRAPH TH
LEVEL 1

Name_____

Sound: /th/
Keywords: the, with

Use a yellow highlighter to color the sound spelling for /th/.

th /th/

Eat more of **that than this.**

Put **both** of **them** in the **bath with** me.

Then they will play.

Fingermapping: Figure 6. TH, EY are one sound. Ex: b-a-th, th-ey.
© 2018 Sarah K Major

DIGRAPH CH
LEVEL 1

Sound: /ch/
Keyword: child

Name_____

Use a yellow highlighter to color the sound spelling for /ch/.

ch /ch/

Put **each**
chop on
your **chin**.

The **chaps** will
chat a bit
and **chow**
much.

The **child** got
such
a **chill**!

Fingermapping: Figures 6-10. EA, CH, OW, LL are one sound.

9

© 2018 Sarah K Major

SHORT E
LEVEL 2

Sound: /ĕ/
Keyword: red

Name_____

Use a yellow highlighter to color the sound spelling for /ĕ/.

e /ĕ/

The **pest** likes to **rest** in the **best nest** in the **west**!

Tell Nell the **bell fell**!

He **bent** the **tent** I **sent**.

He **felt** the **pelt** on his **belt**.

Fingermapping: Figures 4 & 6 (for "tell" etc.)
© 2018 Sarah K Major

SHORT I
LEVEL 2

Sound: /ĭ/
Keyword: it

Name_____

Use a yellow highlighter to color the sound spelling for /ĭ/.

i /ĭ/

I **still**
will
fill
the **grill**
with hotdogs.

I **wish** we had
fish in our
dish!

I **live**
to **give**!

Will **Nick**
pick
Rick to
lick
the **stick**?

Fingermapping: Figure 6. Each ending is 2 letters: LL, SH, VE, CK

© 2018 Sarah K Major

NG & NK
LEVEL 1

Name_____

Sounds: /ng/ /ngk/
Keywords: king, wink

Use a yellow highlighter to color the sound spellings for /ng/ & /ngk/

ng /ng/

The **king** will **ring** for his **wing dings.**

nk /ngk/

Wink at the **pink ink** in the **sink.**

She **rang** and **sang.**

Fingermapping: Figure 6. NG, NK are treated as one sound each.
© 2018 Sarah K Major

SHORT O
LEVEL 2

Sound: /ŏ/
Keywords: on, walk

Name_____

Use a yellow highlighter to color the sound spelling for /ŏ/.

o, *al /ŏ/

My **boss**
will **toss**
the **moss**
across.

We **lost.**
The **frost**
cost us.

The **long**,
song
does not **belong.**
Be **strong!**

I *****walk**
and **talk**
with **chalk.**

*AL sound spelling. Some people pronounce the L in WALK. If you do, teach this sound spelling as just an A.

Fingermapping: SS, NG are one sound. Map multi-syllable words separately: be-long, show 2 fingers then 4 - l-o-ng.

© 2018 Sarah K Major

LONG A
LEVEL 1

Name_____

Sound: /ā/
Keyword: ate

Use a yellow highlighter to color the sound spelling for /ā/.

a-e /ā/

The **tame**,
lame dogs
came
to the **game**
and **ate**.

I will **bake**
a **cake**
to **take**
to the **lake**.

She has **lace**
about her **face**.

A **vase** is
in a **case**
at the **base**.

Fingermapping: all words have four fingers, but the 4th finger represents the Pinchy E. See Section 7, p. xii.
© 2018 Sarah K Major

LONG A
LEVEL 2

Name_____

Sound: /ā/
Keywords: rain, day, they

Use a yellow highlighter to color the sound spellings for /ā/.

ai, ay, ey /ā/

Don't **wait**.
The **rain**
will **stain**
the **daisy**.

I'll put my **bait**
in a **pail**
while I **wait**
for **Gail**.

I **say**,
"Today,
I **may**
stay and
play
all **day**
in the **spray**!"

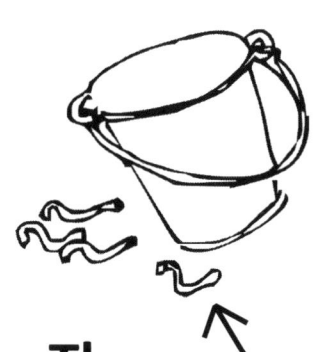

They
are my **prey**.

Fingermapping: Figures 6 & 7. Two letter sounds include: AI, AY, TH, EY

© 2018 Sarah K Major

LONG E
LEVEL 1

Name_____

Sound: /ē/
Keywords: he, see, Pete

Use a yellow highlighter to color the sound spellings for /ē/.

e, ee, e-e /ē/

**He,
me,
she,
(we)** will
be there.

Do you **see?**
I **need**
to **keep**
my **three
feet
green!**

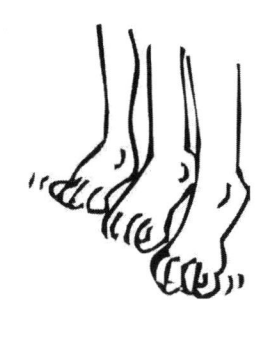

Even here,
Eve and
Pete
lose **these!**

Fingermapping: EE, TH, SH are one sound. Pinchy E, p. xii, Section 7.
© 2018 Sarah K Major
16

FINAL Y
LEVEL 1

Sounds: /ī/ /ē/
Keywords: my, funny

Name_____

Use a yellow highlighter to color the sound spelling for y as /ī/ & /ē/

y /ī/

Try to
pry
my
ply off
the **sty.**

Oh no! It
will **fly**
by in
the **sky.**

y /ē/

I'm **happy**
very
many are
pretty.
Only two
jars of **cherry**
jelly
are **funny.**

Fingermapping: CH, ER, and double letters are two fingers but one sound.

17

© 2018 Sarah K Major

LONG I
LEVEL 1

Name_____

Sound: /ī/
Keywords: find, my

Use a yellow highlighter to color the sound spellings for /ī/.

i, y /ī/

The **child** was **wild**, not **mild**!

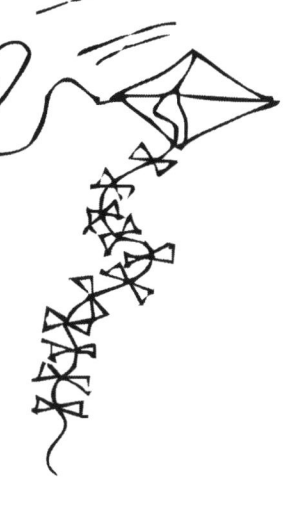

Eeeeeee Yaaaaah!!

I find I don't **mind** if **I'm kind** in a **bind**.

Waah!

My kite goes **by** me in the **sky** when I **try** to **fly** it. That is **why** I will **cry**!

Fingermapping: CH, WH are one sound. Ex: s-k-y, wh-y, ch-i-l-d.

© 2018 Sarah K Major

LONG I
LEVEL 2

Sound: /ī/
Keywords: pie, like

Name_____

Use a yellow highlighter to color the sound spellings for /ī/.

ie, i-e /ī/

I **cried** because
he **tried**
to **tie**
up the **pie**
I'd **fried**!

I got **five**
live
white
mice
while
he was by my
side!

We're **united**!
It's **time** for
you to **like**
your **life**!

Fingermapping: IE, WH are one sound. Ex: f-r-ie-d, wh-i-te. Pinchy E, p. xii, Section 7.

19   © 2018 Sarah K Major

LONG I
LEVEL 3

Name_____

Sound: /ī/
Keyword: high

Use a yellow highlighter to color the sound spelling for /ī/.

igh /ī/

The **sigh** was **high**.

It's not **right** to **fight**!

I caught **sight** of a **bright** **light** in the **night** sky.

I **might** get a **slight** **fright** **tonight**.

Fingermapping: IGH is one sound made of three letters. Ex: s-igh-t.

© 2018 Sarah K Major   20

LONG I
LEVEL 4

Name_____

Sound: /ī/
Keywords: height, eye, island, aisle

Use a yellow highlighter to color the sound spellings for /ī/.

eigh, eye, is, ais /ī/

From his **height,** he could see everything!

An **isle** is an **island**.

An **aisle** is in a church.

I see you with my **eyes!**

Fingermapping: Figure 6, p. x. EIGH, EYE, IS, AIS, LE are each one sound. Ex: h-eigh-t, is-le, is-l-a-n-d.

21

© 2018 Sarah K Major

/L/
LEVEL 1

Name_____

Sound: /l/
Keywords: left, well, fossil

Use a yellow highlighter to color the sound spellings for /l/

l, ll, il /l/

A **lift**
will **land**
me in the **left**
loft where
I will **lie.**

The **pupil**
is **ill.**

I **will**
sell
the **full**
doll in
the **mall**
at the **well.**

Fingermapping: LL, IE are one sound. See Figure 6, p. x.

© 2018 Sarah K Major

LONG O
LEVEL 1

Sound: /ō/
Keyword: go

Name_____

Use a yellow highlighter to color the sound spelling for /ō/.

o /ō/

Oh!
So it's
a **no**
go?

She **told** me
she'd **hold**
my **old**
gold,
but was **cold**
and **bold,**
and **sold** it!

I **also**
don't
want **both.**
Only that one!

Fingermapping: TH is one sound.

23 © 2018 Sarah K Major

LONG O
LEVEL 2

Name_____

Sound: /ō/
Keywords: home, poor

Use a yellow highlighter to color the sound spellings for /ō/.

o-e, oo /ō/

Eat **more*** of the **core** **before** you go to the **store**.

*More about R-Controlled ORE words on page 87.

Please **open** the door, then **close** it, and go **home**!

Still **over** the **smoke** was the **stroke** that **broke** the tree.

The **poor** **floor** is by the **door** to the **moor**!

Fingermapping: OO, ER are one sound. Pinchy E, p. xii, Section 7.

© 2018 Sarah K Major

LONG O
LEVEL 3

Name_____

Sound: /ō/
Keywords: goat, snow

Use a yellow highlighter to color the sound spellings for /ō/.

oa, ow /ō/

A **goat** in a **coat** will **float** on a **soap boat**.

I'll **toast** all the **loaf**.

I'll **show** you the **low glow**.

You **know** I'll **throw** my **own snow below**.

Fingermapping: OA, OW, SH, KN, TH are one sound.

25 © 2018 Sarah K Major

LONG U

Sound: /ū/
Keywords: pupil, use, few, cue

Name_____

Use a yellow highlighter to color the sound spelling for /ū/.

u, u-e, ew, ue /ū/

It is **usual** for a **pupil** to **unite** with friends.

I will **use** a **fuse** to get my **mule** to move.

She will watch for her **cue.**

Only a **few** didn't say **ew!** as they ate the **stew!**

Fingermapping: UE, EW are one sound. Pinchy E, p. xii, Section 7.

© 2018 Sarah K Major   26

/ŌŌ/ LEVEL 1

Sound: /ŌŌ/
Keywords: to, flu, flute

Name_____

Use a yellow highlighter to color the sound spellings for /ŌŌ/.

o, u, u-e /ŌŌ/

Waka waka waka waka...

Do what
to
whom?
I'm into
"Do unto others
today, what you want for yourself."

Sniff!
Cough!

Stu, has the flu.

The truth?
Tulips are lovely!

It was a super flute!

Fingermapping: WH, AY, TH, ER are one sound.

27

© 2018 Sarah K Major

/ŌŌ/
LEVEL 2

Name_____

Sound: /ŌŌ/
Keywords: you, lose, cool, shoe

Use a yellow highlighter to color the sound spelling for /ŌŌ/.

ou, o-e, oo, oe /ŌŌ/

You eat **soup** in a **group!**

Whose did you **lose** when you **moved?**

Mr. **Booth** has **balloons**, a **spoon**, **food**, and **boots**, **too**, but no **tooth!**

The **canoe** is a **shoe!**

Fingermapping: WH, OO, TH, LL, SE, ED, SH are one sound. Fingermap balloons in two syllables: b-a-ll / oo-n-s.

© 2018 Sarah K Major

/ŏŏ/
LEVEL 1

Name_____

Sound: /ŏŏ/
Keywords: put, book

Use a yellow highlighter to color the sound spellings for /ŏŏ/.

u, oo /ŏŏ/

I **put** the **full** **bull** in the wagon.

Me?

Yup!

Now you **push** or **pull** him!

I **took** a **good** **look** at the **cook** **book**.

Fingermapping: LL, SH are one sound.

29 © 2018 Sarah K Major

/OI/
LEVEL 1

Name_____

Sound: /oy/
Keywords: joy, join

Use a yellow highlighter to color the sound spellings for /oi/

oy, oi /oi/

The **boy** gave the **toy** to **Joy** and **Troy.**

I'll **point** to the **coin** in the **soil!**

Let the **oil** **boil** in the **foil.**

Fingermapping: OY, OI are one sound.

© 2018 Sarah K Major

/OW/
LEVEL 1

Sound: /ow/
Keywords: cow, out

Name_____

Use a yellow highlighter to color the sound spellings for /ow/

ow, ou /ow/

**Wow,
how**
the **sow**
will **bow**
to the **cow**
now!

I will go
out and
about
our
house.

Fingermapping: OW, OU, SE are one sound.

31

© 2018 Sarah K Major

/ER/
LEVEL 1

Name_____

Sound: /er/
Keywords: girl, her, worm

Use a yellow highlighter to color the sound spellings for /er/

ir, er, or /er/

Sir,
the **girl**
will **stir**
the **fir.**

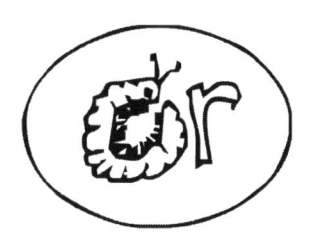

"Or" is a **word**
in **work**
and **worm.**

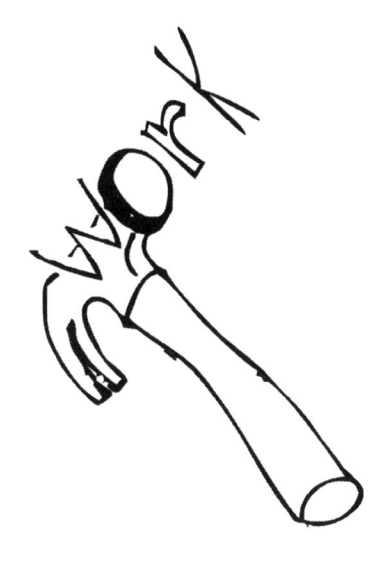

We **were**
to **serve**
her.

Fingermapping: RE, VE endings - 1 sound, 2 fingers. Figure 13, p. xii. ERE in were /ER/.

© 2018 Sarah K Major

/ER/
LEVEL 2

Sound: /er/
Keywords: girl, turn

Name_____

Use a yellow highlighter to color the sound spellings for /er/

ir, ur /er/

The **first** **girl** saw the **third** **bird** in the **dirt**.

It won't **hurt** to **turn** your **fur** in a **curl**.

She had a **shirt** and a **skirt** at the **circus**.

The **surf** will **churn** **during** the storm.

Fingermapping: TH, SH, CH, NG are two fingers but one sound. C-ir-c-u-s, ch-ur-n, d-ur-ing.

© 2018 Sarah K Major

/AR/
LEVEL 1

Name_____

Sound: /ar/
Keywords: star, heart

Use a yellow highlighter to color the sound spellings for /ar/

ar, ear /ar/

Art took the **cart** apart.

Smart Bart had a **tart** one from the **mart.**

Mark saw **stars** in the **park.**

He loves them with all his **heart.**

Fingermapping: Sounds at top of page are one sound but 2-3 fingers.
© 2018 Sarah K Major

/AR/
LEVEL 2

Name_____

Sound: /ar/
Keyword: star

Use a yellow highlighter to color the sound spelling for /ar/

ar /ar/

The **alarm** will **start** the **party.**

Wear your **parka** and **scarf** to **art.**

I'm in **charge.** This **smart army** will **march** to the **market.**

Carla's arms are **large** and **scarlet.**

Fingermapping: AR, CH, GE are one sound. M-ar / k-e-t, s-c-ar / l-e-t.

© 2018 Sarah K Major

/K/
LEVEL 1

Name_____

Sound: /k/
Keywords: cat, kick, kiss

Use a yellow highlighter to color the sound spellings for /k/

c, ck, k /k/

Bad **luck** – when I'm **sick**, I can't **kick**.

I **cast** my **cake** in a **cave**.

I'll **lock** the **rock** by the **dock**.

Take a **look** at the **cook**.

I see a **pike** on a **bike**.

Don't **kiss** the **kite**.

Fingermapping: CK, OO, SS are one sound. Note Pinchy E.

© 2018 Sarah K Major

/K/ & /KW/
LEVEL 2

Sound: /k/ /kw/
Keywords: kick, Chris, kiss, cat, queen

Name_____

Use a yellow highlighter to color the sound spelling for /k/ and /kw/

ck, ch, k, c /k/   qu /kw/

Give it a **quick crack.**

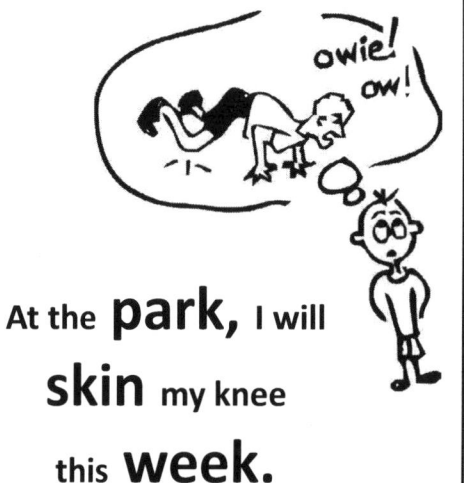

At the **park**, I will **skin** my knee this **week.**

Oh! **Quit,** or the **queen** will give the **quart** a **quick squeeze.**

There was **magic music** at the second **picnic.**

Chris has no **school** at **Christmas.**

Fingermapping: EE, OO, AR, ZE are one sound. Map words by syllable. See p. xii, Section 8.

SHORT E
LEVEL 3

Name_____

Sound: /ĕ/
Keywords: head, said, friend

Use a yellow highlighter to color the sound spellings for /ĕ/.

ea, ai, ie /ĕ/

I **meant** to have **bread** **ready** for **breakfast.**

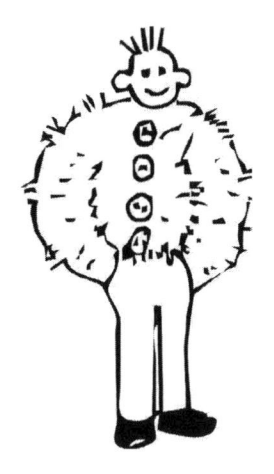

I **spread** the **heavy** **sweater** to dry, **instead** of catching a **head** cold.

We're **friends** to the end!

I **said** **again,** I've been **against** snakes!

I'm outta here!!!

Fingermapping: Figure 7, 10, and 11. EA, AI, IE, ER are one sound. Map compound words separately: b-r-ea-k / f-a-s-t.

© 2018 Sarah K Major

SHORT O
LEVEL 3

Name_____

Sound: /ŏ/
Keywords: saw, want

Use a yellow highlighter to color the sound spellings for /ŏ/.

aw, a /ŏ/

I **saw** the **fawn**
on the **lawn**
yawn at
dawn.

It's the **law**
to **draw**
straws.

**Father,
what** I
want is
water!

I **was** going
to **watch** you
wash the dog.

Fingermapping: AW, TH, WH, TCH, SH, ER are one sound.

SHORT U
LEVEL 2

Name_____

Sound: /ŭ/
Keywords: up, does, other

Use a yellow highlighter to color the sound spellings for /ŭ/.

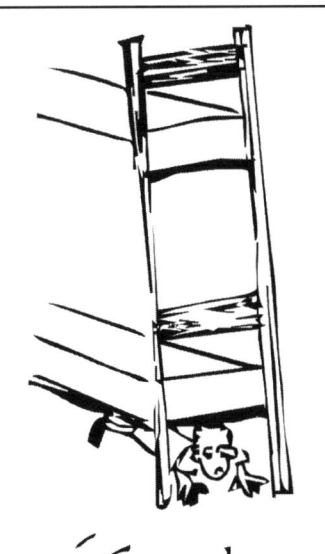

u, oe, o /ŭ/

You **must** stay **under** the **bunk** **until** I say so!

Does it look **done**?

My **mother** and **brother** will go the **other** way.

Some boys will **come** and **shove** me high **above** the **dove** I **love**.

Fingermapping: ER, OE, TH, consonant+E endings are one sound.

© 2018 Sarah K Major

/AIR/
LEVEL 1

Name_____

Sound: /air/
Keywords: where, their, care, pair

Use a yellow highlighter to color the sound spellings for /air/

ere, eir, are, air /air/

Where is it?
There!

Pay the **fare** for the **hare** who will **care** if he's **bare**.

The fir tree* is **their** tree.

The **pair** will take a **chair** to the **fair** and wear their **hair** in the **air** with **flair**.

*"The fir" becomes "their" when you lose the "f" from "fir."

Fingermapping: WH, TH, CH, and sounds at top of page are one sound.

41

© 2018 Sarah K Major

/EAR/
LEVEL 1

Name_____

Sound: /ear/
Keywords: here, deer

Use a yellow highlighter to color the sound spellings for /ear/

ere, eer /ear/

We're
here
in cashmere.

Cheer the
steer!
And don't sneer or
leer
at the deer.

I peer
at the career
pioneer.

Fingermapping: SH, CH, and sounds at top of page are one sound. Silent E, p. xii, Section 8.

© 2018 Sarah K Major

/EAR/
LEVEL 2

Name_____

Sound: /ear/
Keywords: near, pier

Use a yellow highlighter to color the sound spellings for /ear/

ear, ier /ear/

sounds like

I **fear**
the **tear**
is **near**
the **rear**
of the **year.**

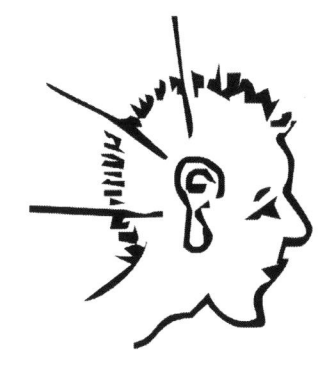

Please, **clear**
your **ear**
so you can **hear.**

I can see it
pierced the
pier!

Fingermapping: ED and sounds at top of page are one sound.

43

© 2018 Sarah K Major

/OR/
LEVEL 1

Name_____

Sound: /or/
Keywords: for, more

Use a yellow highlighter to color the sound spellings for /or/

or, ore /or/

Don't forget.

Do your **chores** **before** you go to the **store**.

This **story** is about a **tortoise** named **Ivory** who was **born** on the **stormy** shore.

Fingermapping: CH, OI, and sounds at top of page are one sound. Silent E, p. xii, Section 8.

/OR/
LEVEL 2

Sound: /or/
Keyword: for, more

Name_____

Use a yellow highlighter to color the sound spellings for /or/

or, ore /or/

The **hornet** stung the **stork** who tore the **acorn** on the **porch**.

The **storm** is in the **north corner** this **morning**.

Don't **forget** to **order** the **form**.

She **tore** what she **wore before** she got to **score more**.

Fingermapping: ER, CH, TH, NG, and sounds at top of page are one sound.

45 © 2018 Sarah K Major

SOFT C & G
LEVEL 1

Sounds: /s/ /j/
Keywords: cent, gel, giant, gym, large

Name_____

Use a yellow highlighter to color the sound spellings for /s/ & /j/

ce /s/

g(e), g(i), g(y)
-ge /j/

Grace will **place** the **lace** about her **face.**

Gem, a **large gentle genie,** wears **gel.**

There's a **giant giraffe** by the **gym.**

Fingermapping: AR, IE, LE, FF are one sound. Silent E, p. xii, Section 8.

© 2018 Sarah K Major

SOFT C & G
LEVEL 2

Sounds: /s/ /j/
Keywords: cent, city, lace, large, fudge

Name_____

Use a yellow highlighter to color the sound spellings for /s/ & /j/

c(e), c(i), -ce /s/

It's **nice**
to **dance**
in the **center**
of the **space**
for **once.**

Draw a **circle**
around the **city**
circus with
your **pencil.**

-ge, dge /j/

The **range**
is **strange.**

I need my **badge**
so I'll **dodge**
to the **lodge**
on the **ridge**
by the **bridge.**

Fingermapping: DG, ER, IR, LE are one sound.

© 2018 Sarah K Major

DOUBLES
LEVEL 1

Name_____

Double consonants

Use a yellow highlighter to color the double consonants in each word.

For **dinner**
or **supper**
in the **summer,**
pepper
is **better!**

He left the **letter**
on the **ladder!**

It was **sudden!**
It did **happen!**
The **kitten**
lost her **mitten!**

Our **lesson**
today is on **cotton**
ribbon.

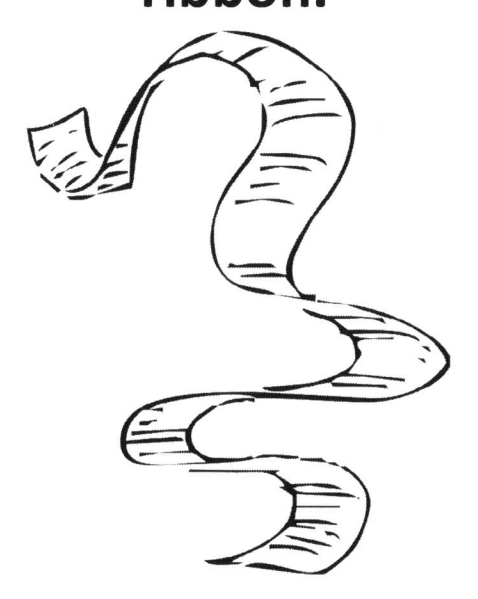

Otto is on the **bottom.**

Fingermapping: double consonants and ER are one sound.

© 2018 Sarah K Major 48

DOUBLES
Level 2

Name_____

Double consonants with short vowels & single consonants with long vowels.

Use a yellow highlighter to color the double consonants in each word. The words with long vowel sounds have only one consonant in the middle of the word. Color the consonant in the middle of the words.

I **grinned** and **tapped** as I **wrapped.**

I'm **grinning** and **tapping** and **wrapping.**

I'm **joking** about **saving** my gum.

I **cared** that she's so **caring** and **smiled** to see her **smiling!**

The rule-breaker!

I **fixed** mine; he's **fixing** his.

Fingermapping: NG, WR, ED, and double consonants are one sound. Fix is a rule-breaker: short vowel with one consonant.

49 © 2018 Sarah K Major

LONG E
LEVEL 2

Name_____

Sound: /ē/
Keywords: see, key, funny, eat

Use a yellow highlighter to color the sound spellings for /ē/.

ee, ey, y, ea /ē/

The **sheep** on **sweet street** have **wheels** of **cheese.**

SWEET STREET

So **many funny** cats **only** come to the **city** to play!

city limits

The **monkey** has the **key** to the **money!**

I'll **eat** my **treat** on a **seat** by the **sea!**

Fingermapping: EE, SH, WH, CH, EY, NN, EA are one sound.

© 2018 Sarah K Major

LONG E
LEVEL 3

Name_____

Sound: /ē/
Keyword: eat

Use a yellow highlighter to color the sound spelling for /ē/.

ea /ē/

Oh **please** let me **dream** that you'll **really leave!**

Bea, please eat your **wheat** with **clean** hands, or you'll **grease** your **pleats!**

Fingermapping: EA, SE, VE, LL, WH are one sound. Silent E, p. xii, Section 8.

51

© 2018 Sarah K Major

LONG O
LEVEL 4

Name_____

Sound: /ō/
Keywords: Joe, your, though

Use a yellow highlighter to color the sound spellings for /ō/.

oe, ou, ough /ō/

A **doe** named **Poe** puts her **toe** on **Joe's** **hoe** as she **goes** by!

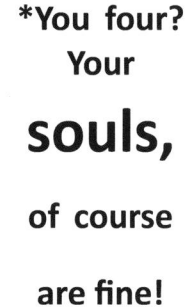

*You **four**? **Your** **souls**, of course are fine!

*See more about OUR spellings on page 80.

*I poured fourteen **potatoes** in the bowl.

Though and **although** are almost the same!

Fingermapping: OE, OU, OUGH, TH, OUGH are one sound. Map multi-syllable words separately: p-o / t-a / t-oe-s.

© 2018 Sarah K Major   52

DIGRAPH TH
LEVEL 2

Name_____

Sound: /th/
Keywords: the, with

Use a yellow highlighter to color the sound spelling for /th/.

th /th/

Yes, **these three** will get **those things!**

Mother and **father together** are **thick,** not **thin.**

I **think** I'll go see if **their** fir tree is still **there.**

The **moth** ate the **other cloth.**

Fingermapping: TH, EE, NG, ER, CK, NK, EIR, ERE are one sound. Map multi-syllable words separately: t-o / g-e / th-er.

© 2018 Sarah K Major

DIGRAPH CH
LEVEL 2

Name_____

Sound: /ch/
Keywords: catch, child

Use a yellow highlighter to color the sound spellings for /ch/.

tch, ch /ch/

Please **watch** that you **match** the **patch** on the **thatch**.

The **stitch** will **itch**, but I can't **scratch** it.

I'll **stretch** to **catch** the ball.

The **etch** a **sketch** is in the **ditch**.

I've a **hunch** the **bench** is in the **trench**.

Fingermapping: TH and spellings at top, center page are one sound.

© 2018 Sarah K Major

DIGRAPH WH
LEVEL 1

Name_____

Sound: /wh/
Keyword: when

Use a yellow highlighter to color the sound spelling for /wh/.

wh /wh/

What hat?
when is Jen coming?
where is her chair?
which whip?
why fly?

are all good question words.

The **whale** is a **whiz** at the **wheel,** I **whined.**

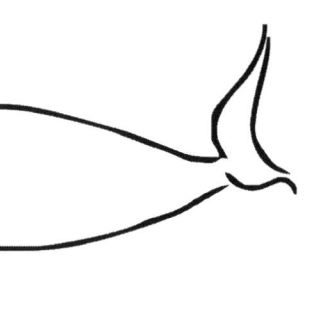

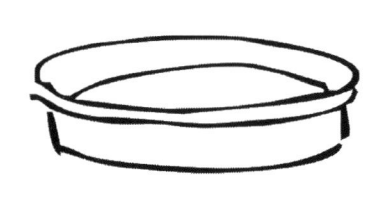

Please **whip** the eggs for the cake.

Fingermapping: WH, CH, EE, ED are one sound. Silent E, p. xii, Section 8.

55 © 2018 Sarah K Major

/ŌŌ/ LEVEL 3

Name_____

Sound: /ŌŌ/
Keywords: suit, new, blue, through

Use a yellow highlighter to color the sound spellings for /ŌŌ/.

ui, ew, ue, ough /ŌŌ/

The **suit** will **bruise** the **fruit**.

you & I
build
You and I will build.
You and I wear suits.
You and I like fruit.
You and I got a bruise.

Drew, there's **new dew** on the **stew!**

Sue, it's **true,** the **clue** was **blue glue.**

The birds **grew,** then **flew.**

I love blue glue!
blue glue

The glue is coming **through!**

Fingermapping: spellings at top of page and SE are one sound.
© 2018 Sarah K Major   56

/ŏŏ/
LEVEL 2

Name_____

Sound: /ŏŏ/
Keywords: book, could

Use a yellow highlighter to color the sound spelling for /ŏŏ/.

oo, oul /ŏŏ/

The **crooked wooden foot** sat on the **woolen** rug.

She **stood** by the **brook** and **shook**. My **goodness**, the **snook** is huge!

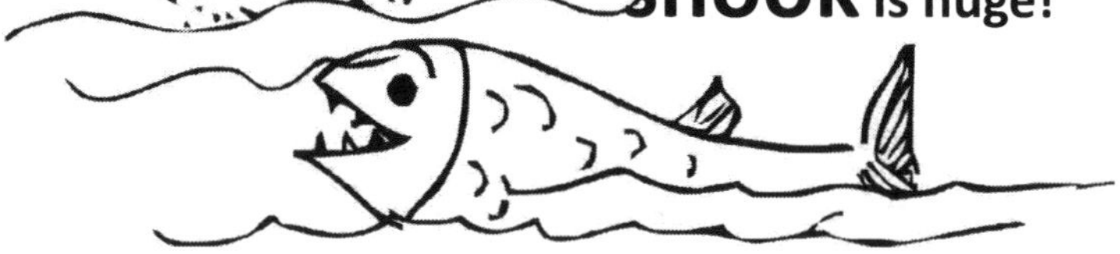

I **would** if I **could**, but you **should** clean up (not me!).

When I **looked**, I **mistook** him for a **crook!**

Fingermapping: SH, SS, ED are one sound. Fingermap by syllables: f-oo-t / s-t-oo-l.

© 2018 Sarah K Major

/OI/
LEVEL 2

Sound: /oy/
Keywords: joy, join

Name_____

Use a yellow highlighter to color the sound spelling for /oi/

oy, oi /oi/

I **enjoy** a **loyal royal**.

Ahoy! Don't **destroy** the **oyster decoy!**

I'll **join** in the **noise!**

His **voice** will **spoil** this **joint**.

I ran to **avoid** the **moist hoist!**

Fingermapping: OY, OI, SE, CE, ER are all one sound.

© 2018 Sarah K Major

/OW/
LEVEL 2

Sound: /ow/
Keywords: cow, out

Name_____

Use a yellow highlighter to color the sound spellings for /ow/

ow, ou /ow/

The **brown clown** will **frown downtown**.

Go **around** the **grounds outside without** me.

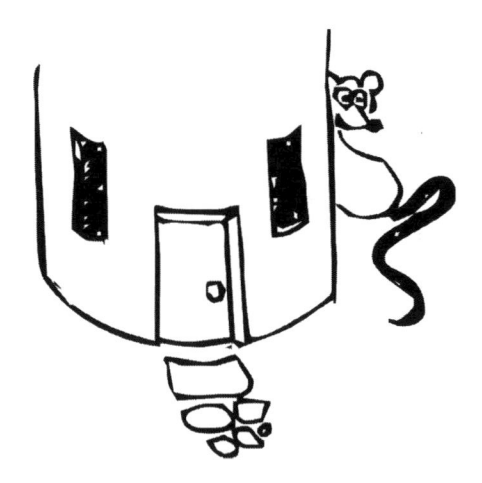

It will **shower** on the **flower**.

I'll give a **shout** when I've **found** the **stout mouse!**

Fingermapping: SH, ER, TH, SE are one sound. Pinchy E, p. xii, Section 8.

/UH/

Sound of schwa /uh/ (letter a sounds like uh)

Name_____

Use a yellow highlighter on the schwa at the beginning of each word.

a /uh/

I see you are **asleep.**
I'm **about** to go out and I'm **afraid** it will rain **again.**

I see the one **above** is **awake.**

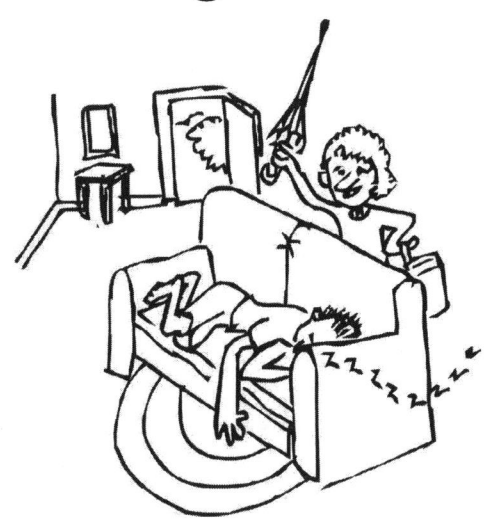

Awhile ago it was **alive.** I saw it go **away-- ahead around** and **about** the barn.

Fingermapping: long vowel spellings and diphthongs are one sound. Also WH, VE, and Pinchy E spellings.

© 2018 Sarah K Major

NG & NK
LEVEL 2

Name_____

Sounds: /ng/ /ngk/
Keywords: king, wink

Use a yellow highlighter to color the sound spellings for /ng/ & /ngk/

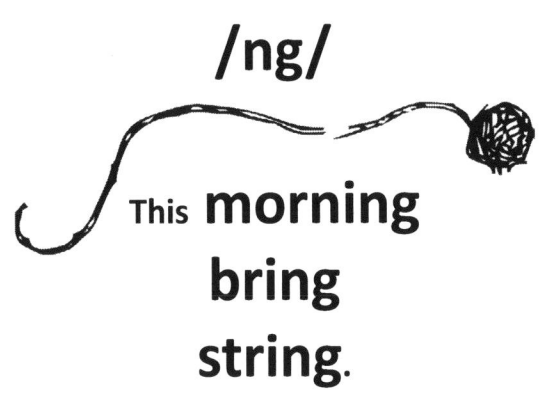

/ng/

This **morning**
bring
string.

I want **nothing**
but a **spring**.

The bee **stung**
her nose as she
hung the wash.

nk /ngk/

I **think**
this **drink**
stinks!

The **bank**
stank and
the **tank**
sank.

The **bunk**
stunk.

Fingermapping: NG, NK, TH are one sound; two fingers for each.

61

© 2018 Sarah K Major

Y as LONG E
LEVEL 2

Name_____

Sound: /ē/
Keyword: funny

Use a yellow highlighter to color the sound spelling for y as /ē/

y /ē/

Every family can **study quickly**.

Sorry! Don't **worry. Larry** can **carry** both the **muddy puppy** and the **funny bunny!** He'll **hurry!** They're **furry**.

The **cherry** is a **merry berry**.

Fingermapping: double letters and CK, ER, QU, CK, CH are two fingers but one sound.

© 2018 Sarah K Major

/ER/
LEVEL 3

Name_____

Sound: /er/
Keywords: curl, worm, learn, her

Use a yellow highlighter to color the sound spellings for /er/

ur, or, ear, er /er/

ur

Okay, **return** the **turkey** or I'll **burst!**

ear

I **heard** and will **learn** about the **early earth** in **earnest!**

her

Remember to **number** your **paper.**

or

Show **vigor!** The **armor** is **worse!**

Fingermapping: EY, SE, AR, and sounds at top of page are 2-3 fingers but one sound.

© 2018 Sarah K Major

/OR/
LEVEL 3

Name_____

Sound: /or/
Keywords: warm, door, your

Use a yellow highlighter to color the sound spellings for /or/

ar, oor, our /or/

My arm was too **warm** in the **war**.

The **poor** **door** is on the **floor**.

The ***tourist** shows **courage** on the **tour**.

Your **fourth** will **pour**.

And, of **course**, your **four** **gourds** are on the **court**!

*See also OUR /ER/ spellings page 82. Depending on pronunciation, teach OUR words as /OR/ or /ER/.

Fingermapping: TH, GE, SE, and sounds at top of page are one sound.

© 2018 Sarah K Major

/F/
LEVEL 1

Name_____

Sound: /f/
Keywords: phone, tough

Use a yellow highlighter to color the sound spellings for /f/

ph, gh /f/

Phil will **phone** for the **photos**.

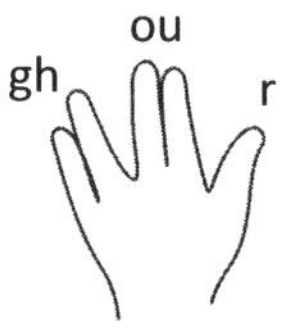

Phew! Phil's phony phase with **phlox** is over!

I am **rough** and **tough enough!**

He will both **laugh** and **cough!**

I see a **phrase** in our **phonics** book.

Fingermapping: PH, EW, GH, AU are 2 letter sound spellings. OU sounds like short O (p. 71) and short U (p. 72).

© 2018 Sarah K Major

/L/
LEVEL 2

Name_____

Sound: /l/
Keywords: little, rural

Use a yellow highlighter to color the sound spellings for /l/

le, al /l/

All the **simple little purple people** love to **sample** a **maple apple.**

Al's **rural sabal** is **natural.**

In **general,** I'm **loyal** to the **final normal rural festival.**

Fingermapping: TT, UR, EO, PP, OY, OR, UR are one sound. Map words a syllable at a time. See p. xii.

/R/
LEVEL 1

Name_____

Sound: /r/
Keywords: rhino, wren

Use a yellow highlighter to color the sound spellings for /r/

rh, wr /r/

A **rhino** has no **rhythm** and can't **rhyme**.

um uh duh

The **wren** will **write** what I **wrote** with the **wrong** **wrist**.

Rhoda left **Rhode** Island for **Rhodesia** to look for a **rhebok**.

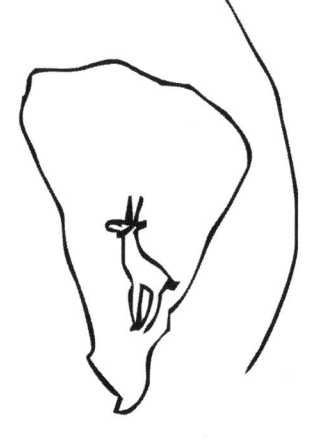

Fingermapping: Section 6 - Letter Clusters, p. xi, and Section 8 - Multi-Syllable Words, p. xii.

67

© 2018 Sarah K Major

PAST TENSE
LEVEL 1

Name_____

Spelling: ed
Sounds: /t/ /d/ /ed/

Use a yellow highlighter to color the sound spellings for /t/, /d/, /ed/

ed /t/, /d/, /ed/

I **tripped**
then **slipped**
and **dropped** it.
So I **stopped**.

She was **charmed**
that I **farmed**.

As I **tilled**,
I **filled** the cart.

I **wanted**
Ed, and I **spotted**
him.

I **rubbed**
as I **planned**.

We **strayed**
as we **played**.

I said it **needed**
to be **weeded**
and **planted**
and **painted**
and **dusted**.
I just **waited**.

Fingermapping: Double letters are one sound. ED /T/ is one sound (t-r-i-pp-ed), ED /D/ (t-i-ll-ed) is one sound.

© 2018 Sarah K Major

PAST TENSE
LEVEL 2

Name_____

Spelling: ed
Sounds: /t/ /d/ /ed/

Use a yellow highlighter to color the sound spelling for /t/, /d/, /ed/

ed /t/, /d/, /ed/

I have **cracked, tracked, chopped,  wrapped, mocked, baked, walked,** and **talked.**

I was busy yesterday! **I cleaned, adored, argued, colored, owned,** and **followed.**

I also **headed, coasted, drifted, boasted, wasted,** and **treated** Ed pretty badly.

Note: The e in "ed" cannot act as "pinchy e" if there are two consonants between it and the vowel (as in "tracked"), nor in the case of "bossy R" ("or" or "er" as in "colored" and "adored"), nor when the previous vowel sound is made of two vowels together as in "treated."

Fingermapping: Double letters are one sound. ED /T/ is one sound, ED /D/ is one sound.

© 2018 Sarah K Major

PLURALS
LEVEL 1

Name_____

Spelling: +s, +es
Sounds: /z/ /ez/

Use a yellow highlighter to color the sound spellings for /z/ & /ez/

+s /z/

The **girls** saw **eggs** turn to **birds**.

Boys in **sneakers** had **boats** and **trucks**.

The **cars** have **firs**.

+es /ez/

She **wishes** for **dishes**, but got **foxes** in **boxes**.

He wears **glasses** in his **classes**.

Fingermapping: Section 6 - Letter Clusters, p. xi.

© 2018 Sarah K Major   70

SHORT O
LEVEL 4

Sound: /ŏ/
Keywords: bought, cough, caught, haul

Name_____

Use a yellow highlighter to color the sound spellings for /ŏ/.

ough, ou, augh, au /ŏ/

I **thought**
they **ought**
to have **brought**
the candy they **bought**
and not have **fought** for more!

I have a **cough!**

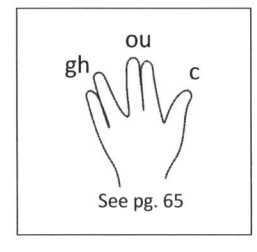

I **caught** and **taught** my **naughty daughter.**

August, said the **author,** is **autumn.**

I **haul** because I like to!

Fingermapping: TH, OUGH, AUGH, ER, AU, MN, SE, OR are one sound. Map by syllable: d-augh / t-er.

71
© 2018 Sarah K Major

SHORT U
LEVEL 3

Name_____

Sound: /ŭ/
Keywords: rough, other, up, flood

Use a yellow highlighter to color the sound spellings for /ŭ/.

ou, o, u, oo /ŭ/

The flood was **rough** and **tough** **enough** to **touch** the whole **country.**

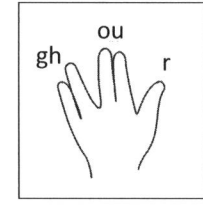

They are **coming,** and **nothing** will stop them!

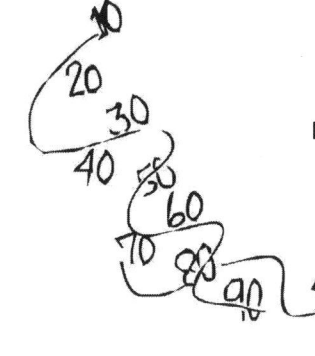

I **understand** my **numbers** to one **hundred.**

There was a **flood** of **blood** when I bumped my nose!

Fingermapping: OUGH, OU, NG, TH, ER, OO are one sound. Map multi-syllable words separately: u-n-d-er / s-t-a-n-d.

© 2018 Sarah K Major

LONG A
LEVEL 3

Name_____

Sound: /ā/
Keywords: rain, day

Use a yellow highlighter to color the sound spellings for /ā/.

ai, ay /ā/

Gail, give us aid with your paintbrush!

The plaintiff was laid in chains.

The mailman on the mainland is unpaid!

Maybe I should always lay the payment away in a tray.

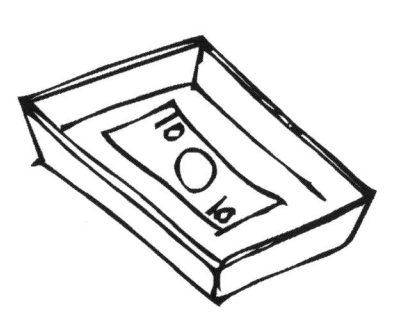

Fingermapping: AI, SH, FF, CH, AY are one sound. Map multi-syllable words separately: p-ai-n-t / b-r-u-sh.

73

© 2018 Sarah K Major

LONG A
LEVEL 4

Name_____

Sound: /ā/
Keywords: break, eight, rein, straight

Use a yellow highlighter to color the sound spellings for /ā/.

ea, eigh, ei, aigh /ā/

Take a **break** for a **great steak!**

The **eight neighbors neigh** at the **weight** of the **freight** in the **sleigh!**

She will **reign,** not **rein.**

In pain, they will go **straight** home!

She's so **vain,** she made a **vane** to show her **vein!**

Fingermapping: EY, EA, EI, EIGH, AIGH, and GN (reign) are one sound. Map by syllable: n-eigh / b-or-s.

© 2018 Sarah K Major

HOMOPHONES
LEVEL 1

Name_____

Homophones

Rely on the sentences to help remember the meaning of each word.

No **way,** not today! I can't **weigh** eight sleighs!

Will you **sell** your bike? The **cell** is in the cellar.

Its leg is broken. **It's** about to sneeze!

It's **great** to eat steak! She ate the cheese I wanted to **grate.**

Gail made a **sail.** Dale had a **sale.**

You **owe** me! **Oh** yeah?

Fingermapping: Section 6 - Letter Clusters, p. xi, and Section 8 - Multi-Syllable Words, p. xii.

© 2018 Sarah K Major

HOMOPHONES
LEVEL 2

Name_____

Homophones

Rely on the sentences to help remember the meaning of each word.

In **here** not there, and I **hear** with my ear.

There they go to see **their** fir tree!

My stew isn't **new**! I **knew** it! It's old!

The skunk left a **scent**.
The **cent** is round.
Selina **sent** me there!

Our dog went out an **hour** ago.

Fingermapping: Section 6 - Letter Clusters, p. xi.

LONG E
LEVEL 4

Name_____

Sound: /ē/
Keywords: chief, ceiling

Use a yellow highlighter to color the sound spellings for /ē/.

ie, ei /ē/

The **thief's** mischief caused **grief** and **relief** to the **chief.**

My **niece** did **achieve.**

I will **shriek** as I **yield** my **shield.**

Next she will **seize** the **protein** and the **caffeine** from the **ceiling.**

Fingermapping: TH, IE, CH, SH, FF, GN are one sound. Also CE, VE, NE endings. A-ch-ie-ve, sh-r-ie-k, c-a-ff-ei-ne.

77

© 2018 Sarah K Major

LONG E
LEVEL 5

Name_____

Sound: /ē/
Keywords: ceiling, people, Maria, petite

Use a yellow highlighter to color the sound spellings for /ē/.

ei, eo, i, i-e /ē/

I **seize** some **leisure** on my **weird ceiling.**

I **receive** the **receipt** with **conceit.**

Oh! So many **people!**

Maria is so **petite!**

Fingermapping: EI, PT, EO are one sound. Also ZE, NG, VE, TE, LE endings. L-ei / s-ure, r-e / c-ei-ve, c-o-n / c-ei-t.

© 2018 Sarah K Major   78

DIGRAPH WH
LEVEL 2

Name_____

Sound: /wh/
Keyword: when

Use a yellow highlighter to color the sound spelling for /wh/.

wh /wh/

Whatever you do,
whisper, don't
whoop,
while I
whittle
the **white**
whistle.

Whenever you
whack
my **whirl**
of **whiskers,**
I **whimper.**

I wonder **whether**
I will catch a
whopper
whitefish.

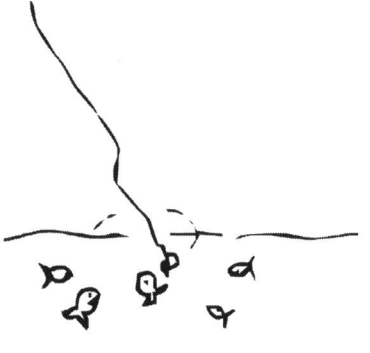

Fingermapping: TH, ER, OO, TT, ST, LE, CK, IR, ER, PP, SH are one sound. wh-e-n / e-v-er, wh-e / th-er.

© 2018 Sarah K Major

/OW/
LEVEL 3

Name_____

Sound: /ow/
Keywords: out, drought

Use a yellow highlighter to color the sound spellings for /ow/

ou, ough /ow/

The **amount** of **flour** in my **mouth** is a **mound**.

I'm **bound** for the **sour mountain**.

There's a **drought** on the mountain.

Can you **pronounce "ounce couch?"**

Fingermapping: TH, AI, ER, CE, CH, LL, AR are one sound. P-r-o / n-ou-n-ce, m-ou-n / t-ai-n.

© 2018 Sarah K Major

/OW/
LEVEL 4

Name_____

Sound: /ow/
Keyword: cow

Use a yellow highlighter to color the sound spelling for /ow/

ow /ow/

We will **plow** through the **crowded vowels**, however, the **prowler** got the **powder**.

I'll **allow** an **allowance** for the **coward** in the **tower**.

Fingermapping: TH, AI, ER, CE, CH, LL, AR are one sound. A-ll-ow / a-n-ce.

/ER/
LEVEL 4

Name_____

Sound: /er/
Keywords: her, learn, tourist, turn

Use a yellow highlighter to color the sound spellings for /er/

er, ear, our, ur /er/

her

I will **insert** my **concern** that he **deserve** the **service**.

ur

Your **murmur** will **further disturb** my **current purpose**.

ear

He will **rehearse** the **search**.

The **tourist** showed **courage** on the **tour**.

Before **curfew** I must **purchase** a **curtain** for my **furnace**.

Fingermapping: AI, CH, RR, CE, SE, GE, VE, TH, and sounds at top of page are one sound.
© 2018 Sarah K Major

/ER/
LEVEL 5

Sound: /er/
Keywords: dollar, syrup, girl, her

Name_____

Use a yellow highlighter to color the sound spellings for /er/

ar, yr, ir, er /er/

I paid a **dollar** for this **collar**!

Oh, and I also got this **syrup**.

I can **confirm** that the **squirrel** will **circulate** around the **circular fir**.

I'm **alert** to **conserve** the **internal** and **external perfume**.

Fingermapping: LL, RR, VE and sounds at top of page are one sound.

83   © 2018 Sarah K Major

/AR/
LEVEL 3

Name_____

Sound: /ar/
Keywords: star, guard

Use a yellow highlighter to color the sound spellings for /ar/

ar, aur /ar/

Pardon my **remark** as I **guard** the **carpet**.

The **apartment** is not **charming**. It is **starting** to be **alarming**.

You may **argue** the **harvest article farther** down. I **regard** my **department**.

Fingermapping: AR, AUR, UA, CH, UE, ER, TH, LE, NG are one sound.

© 2018 Sarah K Major   84

/AIR/
LEVEL 2

Sound: /air/
Keywords: pear, guarantee, care

Name_____

Use a yellow highlighter to color the sound spellings for /air/

ear, uar, are /air/

The **bear** will **wear** the **pear** on his ear.

And we **guarantee** our work!

Waaa!

Does it **scare** you to **share**?

It's **rare** for him to **spare** a **stare**.

Fingermapping: SH and sounds at top of page are one sound. Silent E, p. xii, Section 8.

85   © 2018 Sarah K Major

/AIR/
LEVEL 3

Name_____

Sound: /air/
Keywords: care, pair, vary

Use a yellow highlighter to color the sound spelling for /air/

are, air, ar /air/

air

Don't **despair!**
We will **repair**
with **flair!**

I **declare!**
Are you **aware?**

The **flare**
I **prepare**
for this **area**
will **vary.**

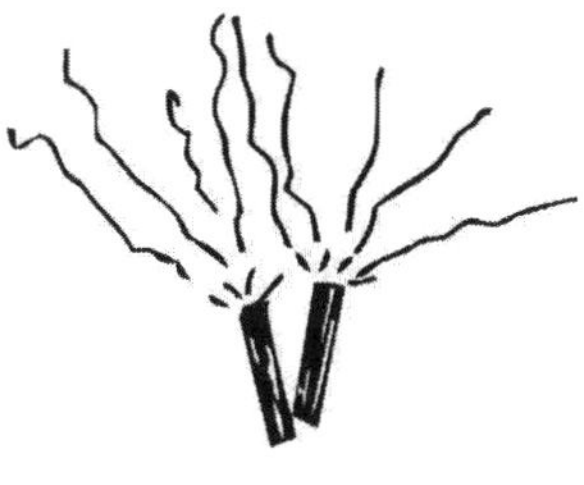

© 2018 Sarah K Major

/OR/
LEVEL 4

Name_____

Sound: /or/
Keywords: for, more

Use a yellow highlighter to color the sound spelling for /or/

or, ore /or/

I **adore**
the **foreman**
with **authority**
over the **territory.**
Therefore,
ignore
my **mortar.**

"or" and "ore" are mixed together.

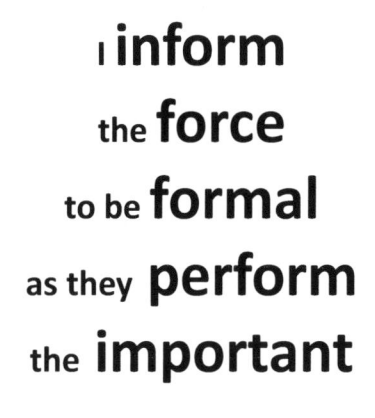

I will **forever**
have the **fortune**
of an **enormous**
ornament.

I **inform**
the **force**
to be **formal**
as they **perform**
the **important**
play.

Fingermapping: TH, AU, RR, ER, OU, AR, CE, NE, OUS, and sounds at top of page are one sound.

87
© 2018 Sarah K Major

Soft C & G
LEVEL 3

Sounds: /s/ /j/
Keywords: cent, cyclops, fudge

Name_____

Use a yellow highlighter to color the sound spellings for /s/ & /j/

c(e), c(y) /s/

The **cell**
in the **cemetery**
has a **ceiling**
of **cement.**

The **cyclops**
has a **cycle** with one
cylinder.

dge /j/

Mercy,
the **cent**
is a **century**
old!

Judge, Bud
will eat **fudge**
as he's **wedged**
in the **hedge**
on the **edge**
of the **ledge.**

Fingermapping: LL, ER, EI, LE, AR, UR, DG are one sound. W-e-dg-ed. Map long words by syllable. C-y / l-i-n / d-er.

© 2018 Sarah K Major

Soft C & G
LEVEL 4

Sounds: /s/ /j/
Keywords: cent, giant, large, gym

Name_____

Use a yellow highlighter to color the sound spelling for soft /s/ & /j/

ce /s/

My **stance** on **France** is that for **romance** they **dance** and **prance.**

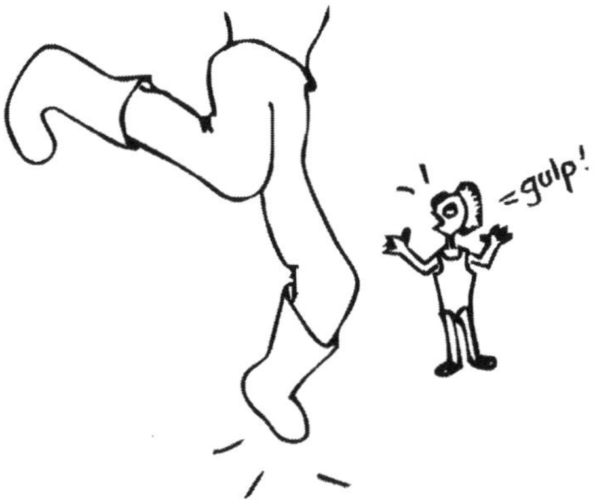

The **gigantic magic giant** does **gymnastics** with the **gymnast.**

g(i), -ge, g(y) /j/

A **package** by the **cottage** was the **cabbage** for the **village.**

I see your **courage** with the **baggage.**

Fingermapping: CK, TT, BB, LL, OUR, GG are one sound. Silent E, p. xii, Section 8. Map long words by syllable.

© 2018 Sarah K Major

/F/
LEVEL 2

Name_____

Sound: /f/
Keyword: off

Use a yellow highlighter to color the sound spelling for /f/

ff /f/

The **traffic** **waffled** and **baffled** me, so an **officer** **offered** to make an **effort** to **effect** a **difficult** change.

No **fun**!
I will **affirm** him!

Fingermapping: FF, ED, ER, OR, IR are one sound.
© 2018 Sarah K Major

/G/

Name_____

Sound: /g/
Keywords: got, baggy, ghost

Use a yellow highlighter to color the sound spelling for /g/

g, gg, gh /g/

Words like **ghastly**, **ghoul**, and **ghost** scare me!

The **baggy gaggle** of geese will **wiggle** and **struggle**.

In the **ghetto** in **Ghana** and **Ghent**[1], people eat **gherkins** dipped in **ghee**[2] while sitting on the **ghat**[3].

The **girls** **got** sick, gave a **great** **groan**, and are **going** home.

1 Ghent: NW Belgium
2 ghee: Indian strained liquid butter
3 ghat: in India, steps to water where people do ritual bathing

Fingermapping: ER, IR, EE, LE, EA, OA, NG are one sound.

91 © 2018 Sarah K Major

/L/ LEVEL 3

Name_____

Sound: /l/
Keywords: parcel, fossil

Use a yellow highlighter to color the sound spellings for /l/

el, il /l/

The **angel** will **counsel** the **panel** to not **marvel** at the **label** on the **parcel**.

The **pupil** took the **fossil** to the **civil** **council**.

Fingermapping: OU, AR, SS are one sound.

© 2018 Sarah K Major

/L/
LEVEL 4

Sound: /l/
Keywords: rural, little

Name_____

Use a yellow highlighter to color the sound spelling for /l/

al, le /l/

My **central rival** is a **typical** gal: **practical, rational** and **neutral.**

An **isle**∗ is a **little** island.

An **aisle**∗ is in a church.

∗is and ais /i/

Fingermapping: Section 6 - Letter Clusters, p. xi, and Section 8 - Multi-Syllable Words, p. xii.

© 2018 Sarah K Major

/M/

Name_____

**Sound: /m/
Keywords: autumn, lamb**

Use a yellow highlighter to color the sound spellings for /m/

mn, mb /m/

Sing an **autumn hymn.**

I'd **comb** my **lamb,** but my **thumb** is **numb.**

We were **solemn** by the **column** where they will **condemn** him.

The **plumber** put the **crumb** in a **tomb** with great **aplomb.**

Fingermapping: Section 6 - Letter Clusters, p. xi, and Section 8 - Multi-Syllable Words, p. xii.

/N/

Sound: /n/
Keywords: know, gnat, pneumonia

Name_____

Use a yellow highlighter to color the sound spellings for /n/

kn, gn, pn /n/

I **know** that my **gnat** has **pneumonia!**

I **knew** that the **knife** was in the **knapsack** by my **knee.**

The **gnat** will **gnaw** on the **gnome.**

I **knit** him some **knickers.**

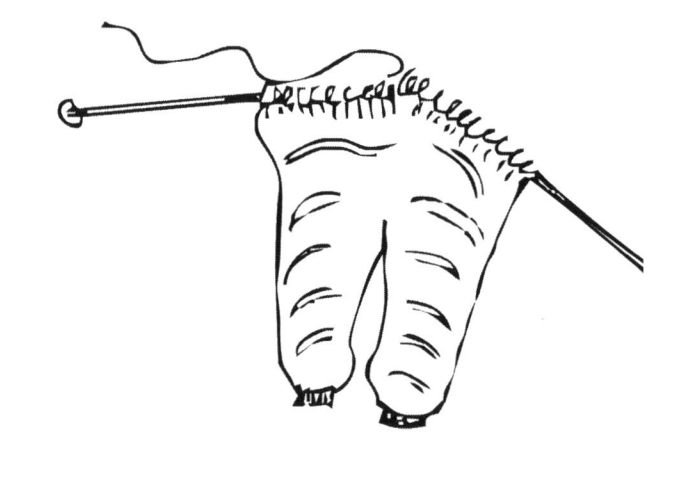

Fingermapping: Section 6 - Letter Clusters, p. xi, and Section 8 - Multi-Syllable Words, p. xii.

© 2018 Sarah K Major

/T/
LEVEL 1

Name_____

Sound: /t/
Keywords: passed, matter

Use a yellow highlighter to color the sound spelling for /t/

ed, tt /t/

I **passed** him the pants I **pressed.**

I'm **putting** a **pretty** **button** on the **kitten's** **mitten.**

I **asked** before I **looked.**

I'll **attempt** to be **attentive** in my **attendance** at school. It **matters**!

Fingermapping: Section 6 - Letter Clusters, p. xi, and Section 8 - Multi-Syllable Words, p. xii.

/z/

Sound: /z/
Keywords: lose, snooze, scissors, his, xylophone

Name_____

Use a yellow highlighter to color the sound spelling for /z/

se, ze, ss, s, x /z/

Phil's new **phase** is to **pause** to **browse**.

The visitor left the **scissors** at school.

If you **lose**, you will **arise** and **tease** each one on the **cruise**.

My **husband** is filled with **optimism** not **pessimism** about **his visitor**.

The **freeze** will **amaze** me so that I can't **snooze**!

The X in **xylophone** sounds like a Z.

Fingermapping: Section 6 - Letter Clusters, p. xi, and Section 8 - Multi-Syllable Words, p. xii.

© 2018 Sarah K Major

OUGH
LEVEL 1

Spelling: OUGH
Sounds: /off/ /uf/ /oh/
Keywords: cough, though, tough

Name_____

Use a yellow highlighter to color the sound spelling for /off/, /uf/, /oh/

ough /off/, /oh/, /uf/

He will **cough** in the **trough.**

Fingermapping: OU-GH sounds like "O-FF"

It's true **though.**
Although I went,
I never got there.

Fingermapping: OUGH sounds like "OH"

He was **rough** and **tough** **enough** to **slough** off all the others.

Fingermapping: OU-GH sounds like "U-FF"

© 2018 Sarah K Major

OUGH
LEVEL 2

Spelling: OUGH
Sounds: /oo/ /ow/ /ŏ/
Keywords: through, bough, thought

Name_____

Use a yellow highlighter to color the sound spelling for /oo/, /ow/, /ŏ/

ough /oo/, /ow/, /ŏ/

The snake crawled **through** the word.

through

Fingermapping: OUGH sounds like "OOO"

The **bough** in the **slough** had a **drought**.

Fingermapping: OUGH sounds like "OW"

Meet the Ought Brothers!

They **thought** they **ought** to have **brought** the candy they **bought** and not have **fought** for more.

Fingermapping: OUGH sounds like short O

PAST TENSE
LEVEL 3

Name_____

Spelling: ed
Sounds: /d/ /ed/

Use a yellow highlighter to color the sound spelling for /t/, /d/ & /ed/

ed /d/, /ed/

They **remained** in the rain and **complained** until they **obtained** umbrellas.

Ed **directed;** what **resulted** is that he **profited.**

We **differed;** he **excelled.**

I **admitted** that I **permitted** it.

I **wondered** who **restored** the **soiled** vase.

Fingermapping: Section 6 - Letter Clusters, p. xi, and Section 8 - Multi-Syllable Words, p. xii.
© 2018 Sarah K Major

PLURALS
LEVEL 2

Spelling: +ies, +s, +es
Sounds: /ĒZ/ /Z/ /S/ /ĔZ/

Name_____

Use a yellow highlighter to color the plural endings.

+ies

I have **memories** of **parties** where I ate **candies** and told **stories**.

My **puppies** eat a lot of **groceries**.

These **diaries** tell of **treaties** with other **countries**.

+s

These **characters** put **essays** in **envelopes**.

The **chiefs** wear **badges** in the **palaces** in the **valleys**.

v+es

The **wolves** cut **loaves** into four **halves**.

Fingermapping: Section 8 - Multi-Syllable Words, p. xii. Map endings: IE-S /ĒZ/, E-S /ĔZ/, V-ES /VZ/

© 2018 Sarah K Major

SPECIAL ENDINGS

Special Endings: n, en

Name_____

Use a yellow highlighter to color the added endings.

+n*

broken
shaken
awaken
stolen
frozen

+en**

frighten
straighten

Double final consonant +en**

flatten
forgotten

---

* Pinchy e makes the first vowel long so you only need to add an n.
Ex: broke > broke**n**.

** Add an en to words which
1) don't have a final e and
2) have multiple final consonants. Ex: fright > fright**en**

*** Must double final consonant + add en if the vowel before final consonant is short. Double consonant will keep the e in en from pinching first vowel. Ex: flat > flat**ten**

Fingermapping: Section 6 - Letter Clusters, p. xi, and Section 8 - Multi-Syllable Words, p. xii.

© 2018 Sarah K Major

SPECIAL ENDINGS

Name_____

Special Endings:
ish, ist, ize

Use a yellow highlighter to color the added endings.

ish, ist, ize

He's acting **childish**, **foolish** and **selfish!**

I know a **scientist** **colonist**, an **artist** **tourist**, and a **typist** **cyclist**.

Her gown is **bluish** and **stylish**.

I **realize** I need to **organize**, **memorize**, **specialize** and **summarize**, so don't **criticize** as I **civilize** and **fertilize** this farm.

Fingermapping: Section 6 - Letter Clusters, p. xi, and Section 8 - Multi-Syllable Words, p. xii.

SPECIAL ENDINGS

Special Endings
sure /zhur/
ture /cher/

Name_____

Use a yellow highlighter to color the added endings.

sure /zhur/

What a **pleasure** to, at **leisure**, **measure** the **treasure**.

ture /cher/

Go **gesture** and **posture** about **nature** in the **pasture**.

Your new **adventure** is to **capture** the **future furniture structure**.

Fingermapping: Section 6 - Letter Clusters, p. xi, and Section 8 - Multi-Syllable Words, p. xii.
© 2018 Sarah K Major

SPECIAL ENDINGS

Special Endings
cia, tia /shu/
sia /zhu/

Name_____

Use a yellow highlighter to color the added endings.

cia, tia /shu/

Marcia made **Patricia** a **facia** for her shop.

sia /zhu/

Asia went to **Persia** to buy a **freesia**, but got **amnesia** instead.

The **consortia's inertia** was due to **dementia.**

Fingermapping: Section 6 - Letter Clusters, p. xi, and Section 8 - Multi-Syllable Words, p. xii.

HOMOPHONES
LEVEL 3

Name_____

Homophones

Rely on the sentences to help remember the meaning of each word.

The **principal's principle** is to not be a pal.

The coat is made of **coarse** cloth. Of **course** it itches.

The **vane** is in the lane.
This **vein** is in my arm.
She's **vain** until she's in the rain!

Wait! I need the **weight** of 8 sleighs!

The **capitol** building is in the **capital** city of Alabama.

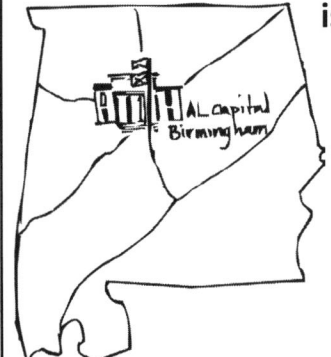

Colin the **Colonel** ate a **kernel** of corn with Kermit and Nel.

Fingermapping: Section 6 - Letter Clusters, p. xi, and Section 8 - Multi-Syllable Words, p. xii.

SHORT I
LEVEL 3

Sound: /ĭ/
Keywords: it, certain, myth, build

Name_____

Use a yellow highlighter to color the sound spelling for /ĭ/.

i, ai, y, ui /ĭ/

My **sister**
will **shiver**
if there's a **sliver**
of **liver**
in the **river**!

that's liver

Captain is
certain to be
on the **mountain**.

That I have **rhythm** in
my **system** is a
myth!

We will **build** again
what we **built** before.

Fingermapping: ER, OU, AI, RH, TH, UI are one sound. Map multi-syllable words separately.

© 2018 Sarah K Major

DIGRAPH SH
LEVEL 2

Name_____

Sound: /sh/
Keywords: sure, machine, she

Use a yellow highlighter to color the sound spelling for /sh/.

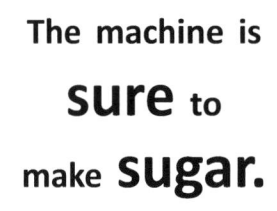

s, ch, sh /sh/

The machine is **sure** to make **sugar**.

She gave a **short shout** at the **shoe show**.

I **shall** get **sharp shears** for **shaving**.

© 2018 Sarah K Major　　108

DIGRAPH SH
LEVEL 3

Sound: /sh/
Keywords: assure, machine, special

Name_____

Use a yellow highlighter to color the sound spellings for /sh/.

ss, ch, ci /sh/

I **assure** you, the **issue** is there's no **tissue** for the **session**.

Patricia made a **special, delicious** treat.

The **chef** has a **chic machine** in the **chalet**.

Fingermapping: Map multi-syllable words separately: P-a / t-r-i / ci-a, s-p-e / ci-a-l, d-e / l-i / ci-ou-s (see p. 136).

109 © 2018 Sarah K Major

/ŌŌ/
LEVEL 4

Name_____

Sound: /ŌŌ/
Keywords: cool, flute

Use a yellow highlighter to color the sound spelling for /ŌŌ/.

oo, u-e, /ŌŌ/

Mr. **Booth** said, "I have **proof.**

A **tablespoon** is bigger than a **teaspoon.**"

I **assume** you will **introduce** me before you **conclude.**

My **attitude** is one of **gratitude.**

Fingermapping: OO, TH, -LE, EA, SS, ME, CE, ME, CE, TT, DE are one sound. Silent E, p. xii, Section 8.

© 2018 Sarah K Major

/ŌŌ/ LEVEL 5

Sound: /ŌŌ/
Keywords: through, you, lose, flu

Name_____

Use a yellow highlighter to color the sound spelling for /ŌŌ/.

ough, ou, o-e, u /ŌŌ/

I'll go **through** my **routine** for the **group.**

Do you **approve** my **moves?**

Yes, your moves are very **fluid.**

Can you **disprove** that I'm good?

I can **remove** any idea that you need to **improve.**

/OI/
LEVEL 3

Sound: /oy/
Keyword: joy

Use a yellow highlighter to color the sound spelling for /oi/

oy /oi/

His **employment**
was an **annoyment**
to the **royalty**
on the **voyage.**

His yak will
destroy
their
enjoyment.

The **destroyer** just
deployed.

Fingermapping: NN, GE, ER, ED. Separate long words into syllables.

/OI/
LEVEL 4

Name_____

Sound: /oy/
Keyword: join

Use a yellow highlighter to color the sound spelling for /oi/

oi /oi/

There's **moisture** in the **adjoining cloister**!

The **boistrous** snake is **poisonous**!

One **factoid**: This **joint** was your **choice**!

I'll **disappoint** you if I **embroider** this.

113

© 2018 Sarah K Major

DOUBLES
LEVEL 3

Name_____

Double consonants

Use a yellow highlighter to color the double consonants in each word.

I will **affirm** that I can **afford** to **affix** a stamp.

She will **assert** her ability to **assemble** an **assortment** of **assets**.

According to this **account**, we have the **assurance** of our **accustomed** payment.

Fingermapping: double consonants, vowel teams, and R controlled spellings are one sound. Silent E, p. xii, Section 8.

DOUBLES
LEVEL 4

Double consonants

Name_____

Use a yellow highlighter to color the double consonants in each word.

I will be **attentive**

to my **attire**

as I **attempt**

to **attain** the prize.

I **applaud**

in my **approval**

to his **application**

at the **appliance** store.

He has the **appetite**

for this work.

/F/
LEVEL 3

Name_____

Sound: /f/
Keywords: phone, tough

Use a yellow highlighter to color the sound spelling for /f/

ph, gh /f/

Play the **phonograph** for the **elephant** at the **pharmacy**.

Pharaoh saw a **phantom** **pheasant**[2] by **Pharos**![1]

1 Pharos: an ancient lighthouse built on the island of Pharos.
2 pheasant, philomels, & phoebes: are birds.

I have a **phobia** about **philomels**[2] and **phoebes**[2].

Fingermapping: PH, GH are one sound. Also OH, OE, EA. Map words a syllable at a time.

© 2018 Sarah K Major

/F/
LEVEL 4

Sound: /f/
Keyword: phone

Name_____

Use a yellow highlighter to color the sound spelling for /f/

ph /f/

The **physician** needs more **phloem**[1] for the **pharmacy**.

The **pamphlet** was about **phonemes**[2] and **graphemes**[3]

1 phloem: part of trunk that carries food to the rest of the tree.
2 phonemes: are the sounds that make up words.
3 graphemes: are the symbols (letters) that represent sounds.

Orpheus, the **orphan sophomore**, had an **epiphany**.

Now he will **triumph** musically!

Fingermapping: PH is one sound. Also OE, EA. Map words a syllable at a time.

© 2018 Sarah K Major

/R/
LEVEL 2

Name_____

Sound: /r/
Keywords: rhino, wren

Use a yellow highlighter to color the sound spelling for /r/

rh, wr /r/

At the **Rhyne**, she saw a **rhesus** with **rheumatism** digging up **rhizomes**.

To **wrangle** means to argue with **wrath**.

Rhetoric and **rhapsody** go well together.

The **wringer** will **wrinkle** the pants.

Fingermapping: Section 6 - Letter Clusters, p. xi, and Section 8 - Multi-Syllable Words, p. xii.
© 2018 Sarah K Major

/R/
LEVEL 3

Sound: /r/
Keyword: rhino, wren

Name_____

Use a yellow highlighter to color the sound spelling for /r/

rh, wr /r/

Her garden is a **rhombus** where she planted **rhododendrons** and **rhubarb**.

Mr. **Wright**, a **wrangler**, got a **wrench** to fix the **wretched wreck**.

The **wraith** will **wrestle** with the **wrapping** on the **wreath**.

Fingermapping: Section 6 - Letter Clusters, p. xi, and Section 8 - Multi-Syllable Words, p. xii.

119

© 2018 Sarah K Major

/s/ LEVEL 1

Name_____

Sound: /s/
Keywords: whistle, scent

Use a yellow highlighter to color the sound spelling for /s/

st, sc /s/

Listen!
She will **whistle**
but her **bustle**
will **rustle**
in the **castle.**

There are **scent** and **scissors** in **science.**

On the **Scilly** Isles the **scion** has a **scimitar** that **scintillates** in the sun.

Fingermapping: Section 6 - Letter Clusters, p. xi, and Section 8 - Multi-Syllable Words, p. xii.
© 2018 Sarah K Major   120

/S/ LEVEL 2

Name_____

Sound: /s/
Keywords: cent, city, cyclops, horse

Use a yellow highlighter to color the sound spelling for /s/

ce, ci, cy, se /s/

They **conceal** the **cereal** and **celery** at the **grocery** store.

Practice to **recite** at the **cinema.**

"CE" and "CI" spellings.

Let's **celebrate** your **recent exercise.**

"CE" and "CI" spellings.

The **cyclops** has a **fancy cylinder.**

He says a **horse** is **worse!**

Fingermapping: Section 6 - Letter Clusters, p. xi, and Section 8 - Multi-Syllable Words, p. xii.

121

© 2018 Sarah K Major

/T/
LEVEL 2

Sound: /t/
Keywords: doubt, pterodactyl

Name_____

Use a yellow highlighter to color the sound spelling for /t/

bt, pt /t/

I **doubt**
he will be **subtle**
about **debt**.

Ptolemy[3] drank
ptisan[4] and got
ptomaine[5]
poisoning and then
ptosis[6].

The **ptarmigan**[1]
and **pterodactyl**
are friends who eat
pteropods[2].

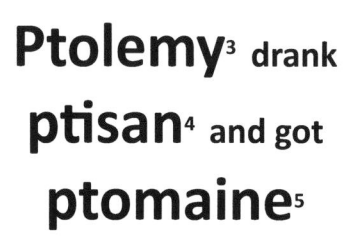

1 ptarmigan: an alpine grouse
2 pteropod: small shell-less gastropod that swims by means of winged lobes
3 Ptolemy: a man who thought that the solar system rotated around the earth
4 ptisan: a drink made of barley
5 ptomaine: foul smelling nitrogenous substances produced by decaying protein
   ptomaine poisoning is an old term for food poisoning
6 ptosis: the falling of an organ, such as a droopy eye

Fingermapping: Section 6 - Letter Clusters, p. xi, and Section 8 - Multi-Syllable Words, p. xii.
© 2018 Sarah K Major

PLURALS
LEVEL 3

Name_____

Plurals

Use a yellow highlighter to color the plural endings.

s inside

The
passers-by
are **mothers-in-law**
and **fathers-in-law.**

s outside

The **mix-ups** were
about **teaspoonfuls,**
spoonfuls
and **cupfuls.**

Fingermapping: Section 6 - Letter Clusters, p. xi, and Section 8 - Multi-Syllable Words, p. xii.

© 2018 Sarah K Major

PLURALS
LEVEL 4

Name_____

Plurals

Use a yellow highlighter to color the plural endings.

__o --> es

The **mosquitoes** love the **potatoes** and **tomatoes** that grow by the **volcanoes**.

f --> v-es

The **shelves** were full of **knives** the **thieves** didn't see.

y --> ie-s

The **opportunities** for **activities** in **companies** have no **boundaries**.

Fingermapping: Section 6 - Letter Clusters, p. xi, and Section 8 - Multi-Syllable Words, p. xii.

SPECIAL ENDINGS

Special Endings: er

Name_____

Use a yellow highlighter to color the added endings.

er

The **passenger**

is either a **commander,**

or a **pitcher**
and **publisher,**

or a **homemaker/ gardener.**

Fingermapping: Section 6 - Letter Clusters, p. xi, and Section 8 - Multi-Syllable Words, p. xii.

SPECIAL ENDINGS

Special Endings: or

Name_____

Use a yellow highlighter to color the added endings.

or

Actor /
Director

Instructor /
Professor

Inventor /
Operator

Editor /
Creditor

The **mayor,**
senator,
and **governor**
love to **motor.**

Fingermapping: Section 6 - Letter Clusters, p. xi, and Section 8 - Multi-Syllable Words, p. xii.

SPECIAL Endings

Special Endings:
ion, ian

Name_____

Use a yellow highlighter to color the added endings.

ion /un/

My **profession**
is a **companion**
with a **solution**
I can **mention.**

My **mission**
is to **section**
a **million** onions.

ian /an/

The **librarian**
has a **comedian**
for a **custodian.**

The **electrician**
is a **guardian**
to the **musician.**

Fingermapping: Section 6 - Letter Clusters, p. xi, and Section 8 - Multi-Syllable Words, p. xii.

SPECIAL
Endings

Special Endings:
sion /zhun/
tion, sion, cian /shun/

Name_____

Use a yellow highlighter to color the added endings.

sion /zhun/

The **vision**
on **television**
was a **collision**,
then an **emersion**.

tion, sion, cian /shun/

Our **mission**
is **suspension**
in another **dimension**.

I'm on **vacation**
at a **plantation**
to get an **explanation**
of the **election**
in our **nation**.

Yes! See I that Ann is a
physician
and a **musician**.

Fingermapping: Section 6 - Letter Clusters, p. xi, and Section 8 - Multi-Syllable Words, p. xii.

SPECIAL Endings

Special Endings:
ment, ate, ness

Name_____

Use a yellow highlighter to color the added endings.

ment, ate, ness

To my **amusement** the **argument** was over my **employment arrangement**.

The **ultimate** cure was **unfortunate**, but it *was* **immediate**.

You're **accurate**. I'm **desolate** and **desperate**.

I love the **swiftness** of his **gentleness** in her **sickness**.

It's **fortunate** that he'll **moderate** the **delicate** meeting.

Fingermapping: Section 6 - Letter Clusters, p. xi, and Section 8 - Multi-Syllable Words, p. xii.

SPECIAL
Endings

Name_____

Special Endings: ant

Use a yellow highlighter to color the added endings.

ant

The **tenant**
is a **servant**
of the **assistant**
to the **attendant**
of the **lieutenant**.

The **applicant**
saw the **participant**
merchant.

The **vacant**
house was **radiant**
and **pleasant**.

Fingermapping: Section 6 - Letter Clusters, p. xi, and Section 8 - Multi-Syllable Words, p. xii.

SPECIAL
Endings

Name_____

**Special Endings:
ent, eer**

Use a yellow highlighter to color the added endings.

ent, eer

I am **confident**
it is no **accident**
that the **superintendent**
is the **ardent**
opponent
of the **resident**
president.

The **volunteer**
engineer
is a **career**
sonneteer
and can **outsteer**
any **pioneer**
or **mountaineer.**

SPECIAL
Endings

Special Endings:
ity, ty

Name_____

Use a yellow highlighter to color the added endings.

ity, ty

For the **majority** of **humanity**, **humidity** hurts their **vanity**.

She has the **ability** to use her **creativity** to make an **activity** that needs **agility**.

Fealty and **loyalty**... each is my **specialty**.

Fingermapping: Section 6 - Letter Clusters, p. xi, and Section 8 - Multi-Syllable Words, p. xii.
© 2018 Sarah K Major
132

SPECIAL
Endings

Name_____

Special Endings: ary

Use a yellow highlighter to color the added endings.

ary

It's **necessary**
to have a **momentary**
voluntary rest.

I'm not **solitary;**
I've an **ordinary**
imaginary friend.

It's **customary**
to have a **temporary**
honorary
secondary backup.

Fingermapping: Section 6 - Letter Clusters, p. xi, and Section 8 - Multi-Syllable Words, p. xii.

SPECIAL
Endings

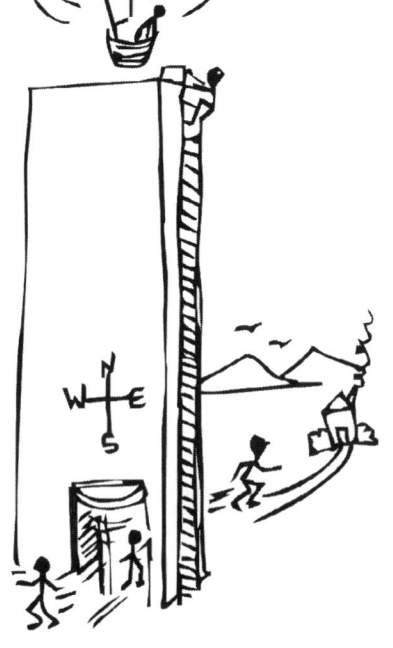

Name_____

Special Endings: ally, ly, ward

Use a yellow highlighter to color the added endings.

ally, ly, ward

Ideally, Ally will have an idea for a fin **finally.** **Additionally,** she'll be **especially** quick to make it.

I'm tired! I went **outward, inward, upward, skyward,** even, and **afterward** went **eastward** and finally **homeward!**

We are **barely** awake, but **loosely,** not **carefully,** we're running **directly** home, **scarcely** seeing it will **certainly** rain. **Possibly** we will be **completely** wet!

Fingermapping: Section 6 - Letter Clusters, p. xi, and Section 8 - Multi-Syllable Words, p. xii.

© 2018 Sarah K Major

SPECIAL Endings

Special Endings: ous /us/

Name_____

Use a yellow highlighter to color the added endings.

ous /us/

It was **marvelous** to hear the **humorous**, **famous** actor talk of his **vigorous**, **dangerous**, **adventurous** trips in **wondrous** **mountainous** lands.

It was **fabulous** not to be **jealous**. I'd be **nervous** in **various** **tremendous** and **horrendous** climbs on **stupendous** mountain peaks.

Fingermapping: Section 6 - Letter Clusters, p. xi, and Section 8 - Multi-Syllable Words, p. xii.

SPECIAL
Endings

Special Endings:
cious, scious, tious /shus/
xious/kshus/

Name_____

Use a yellow highlighter to color the added endings.

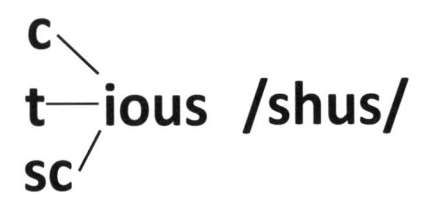

c
t —ious /shus/
sc

xious /kshus/

I see, I owe you s
cious

xious

It was **precocious, malicious, atrocious,** and **ferocious,** to say this is **delicious** and then remain **conscious.**

Better to be **anxious** than **obnoxious.**

Tea I owe you
tious

It is **fictitious** that this is **nutritious.**

Teach the phrase "I owe you" (IOU) to help students remember the spelling pattern. Once those spelling patterns are identified, the rest of the sounds are simple.

Fingermapping: Section 6 - Letter Clusters, p. xi, and Section 8 - Multi-Syllable Words, p. xii.

SPECIAL Endings

Name_____

Special Endings:
ious /eeus/ /shus/

Use a yellow highlighter to color the added endings.

ious /eeus/, /shus/

I'm **contagious,**
but **industrious**
and **studious**
as I work on the **tedious**
lessons.
It's **obvious**
that **various**
curious
fellows are **cautious**
about the class.

On a **precious,**
glorious
Saturday they'd be **furious**
to have to study.

Mom says this **mysterious**
soup is **nutritious.** Hmm.

NOTES:
tious and cious sound like "shus."

Vowels in this ending spell out
"I owe you."
i o u

Fingermapping: Section 6 - Letter Clusters, p. xi, and Section 8 - Multi-Syllable Words, p. xii.

137   © 2018 Sarah K Major

SPECIAL Endings

Special Endings:
eous /ē-ŭs/
uous /ū-ŭs/

Name_____

Use a yellow highlighter to color the added endings.

eous /ē-ŭs/   uous /ū-ŭs/

eous /ē-ŭs/

It is **advantageous** to be **gorgeous, courteous,** and **courageous.**

uous /ū-ŭs/

The line of cars is **congruous** and **continuous.** The climb is **arduous** and the **impetuous** conductor was **ambiguous** about his speed.

Fingermapping: Section 6 - Letter Clusters, p. xi, and Section 8 - Multi-Syllable Words, p. xii.

© 2018 Sarah K Major